More Praise for *Flat Tax Revolution*

❝ With this book, Steve Forbes has once again proven himself to be an indispensable voice in the debate over America's economic future. With big government Republicans and Democrats controlling Washington, Mr. Forbes's visionary reforms are needed now more than ever. **❞**

—JOE SCARBOROUGH
Host of MSNBC's Scarborough Country

❝ When it comes to forecasting what we need to do to keep America's economy growing, Steve Forbes is the answer man. His great new book *Flat Tax Revolution* shows how we can make every American's life more productive, less burdened by bureaucracy, and better off financially. Who can argue with that? If you buy his book, you'll know effectively how to argue for it. **❞**

—JACK KEMP

❝ Steve Forbes challenging the federal income-tax code is like David challenging Goliath. Taxpayers will be happy to learn that in *Flat Tax Revolution* Forbes has let loose the well-aimed stone that can bring the monster down. **❞**

—TERENCE P. JEFFREY
Editor, HUMAN EVENTS

PLEASE VISIT

www.ChooseFlatTax.com

TO LEARN MORE ABOUT THE BOOK

Flat Tax Revolution

Flat Tax Revolution

USING A POSTCARD TO ABOLISH THE IRS

STEVE FORBES

Since 1947
REGNERY
PUBLISHING, INC.
An Eagle Publishing Company • Washington, DC

ISBN 0-89526-040-9

Published in the United States by
Regnery Publishing, Inc.
An Eagle Publishing Company
One Massachusetts Avenue, NW
Washington, DC 20001

Manufactured in the United States of America.

To the "sibs"
Bob
Kip
Tim
Moira

Contents

ACKNOWLEDGMENTS

My saintly wife—and each of our five daughters—uncomplainingly put up with Dad and the seemingly endless gestation period for this book. I wish I could find the words that would adequately express my profound appreciation for their understanding of and encouragement for, this project.

In working with Regnery and with others, Bill Dal Col was instrumental in turning this book idea into a reality.

Special thanks to Regnery, which never hesitates to champion new ideas even when they are controversial. President of Eagle Publishing Jeff Carneal quickly saw the need for this book; Anne Sorock proved to be an enormously able, ever-patient editor; and Regnery President and Publisher Marji Ross was invaluable in bringing the project to completion.

Christian Pinkston of Pinkston Group and his colleagues, Derek Sarley and Aaron Groen, did all—and more—of what I asked of them. Aaron, especially, stoically coped with my never-ending requests.

Highly respected economist and former Treasury officer, Gary Robbins, did the "numbers work" on what impact the Forbes Flat Tax would have on the economy and on the federal budget. Gary and his wife, Aldona, founded Fiscal Associates, which has won renown for sophisticated analyses of how tax changes affect the economy in the real world. Gary's numbers positively and powerfully prove how well the flat tax works.

Veteran tax expert Dan Mitchell of the Heritage Foundation kindly provided invaluable input and advice. Few individuals know this terrain as well as he does. And I am grateful to the other assistance received from the Heritage Foundation, on whose board I sit, including that from chief Ed Feulner and his colleagues, John Von Kannon and Bill Beech.

My deepest appreciation to Merrill Vaughn whose long experience in editing my copy at *Forbes* helped her bring coherence and clarity to the early drafts. I must also thank Scott Bistayi, Elizabeth Gravitt, and Jill Shea for their help in digging up various facts. Special acknowledgement must go to Creative Response Concepts, particularly to Greg Mueller and Peter Robbio for their insight and savvy.

Without the essential assistance of Jackie DeMaria and Maureen Murray, this book would never have come to pass.

And special thanks to Elizabeth Ames whose flair for editing and organizing was absolutely invaluable in enlivening the text ahead.

An Idea Whose Time Has Come

NEWT GINGRICH

MAY 25, 2005

This book is important for you, your family, and your country. You should read it carefully and apply its principles to assessing your own tax situation and evaluating how much better off you would be under a flat tax system.

Steve Forbes has done a great service for all Americans.

In one slim volume he has packed more information about the advantages of a flat tax and the disadvantages of the current tax system than I have ever seen in one place.

Steve draws on a quarter century of academic research by Alvin Rabushka and others. He combines that intellectual knowledge with practical reporting about countries across the planet that have improved their economies by moving to a flat tax system.

Steve Forbes has gone beyond mere reporting and analyzing to a creative proposal of great power. The new Steve Forbes Flat Tax is a reform idea that will translate into a tax cut for every American while also adding seven to ten percent to the American economy through faster economic growth.

That would add $800 billion to $1.2 trillion 200 billion in extra economic activity within just a few years of implementing a flat tax.

This extra economic growth would help finance the transition to a personal social security savings account system, help balance the federal budget, increase philanthropic giving to charities, increase business investment in new machines and new technology so American workers could compete successfully in the world market and, finally, this growth would increase your take home pay, your family's retirement savings, and your ability to achieve dreams of a better future.

The ability of a flat tax to accelerate economic growth and increase your personal quality of life is actually understated by looking only at tax numbers.

As Steve Forbes makes abundantly clear, the number of dollars and hours Americans spend in record keeping and in filling out tax forms is an additional tax burden that drains our economy and drains our personal lives. The hours we spend on IRS minutiae are hours we could spend with our children and our friends. The hours we spend worrying over the complicated and almost incomprehensible tax forms are hours we could be spending on our favorite hobbies.

The Forbes Flat Tax is more than a big idea. It is the right idea and it is a doable idea.

In 1994 we signed a Contract with America. That Contract led to the first comprehensive welfare reform in sixty years, a balanced budget for four consecutive years, the first tax cut in sixteen years, and a host of other reforms.

The Contract with America worked because the American people wanted it to work. In town hall meetings, on talk radio, in letters to the editor, in meetings with their congressman and senators, Americans insisted on real change and demanded the implementation of the key promises in the Contract.

I believe there is a real opportunity for a similar grass roots revolution imposing the flat tax on Washington. As people learn how much money and time they can save through a flat tax they are going to demand a simple alternative to the complexity and uncertainty of the Internal Revenue Service. As people spend hours in frustrating and seemingly endless paperwork and record keeping and preparing they are going to demand the freedom for their own time offered by a flat tax. As people contemplate the challenges of China and India in job creation and economic growth they are going to demand the extra growth made possible by the flat tax. As people watch the endless maneuvering of the lobbyists and the special interests they are going to demand the fairness of a flat tax.

Read this book.

Get your friends to read this book.

Every time someone complains about taxes, get them to read this book.

Together we can help America and help ourselves.

That is the opportunity Steve Forbes has created for all of us.

"The difficulty lies, not in the new ideas, but in escaping from the old ones, which ramify, for those brought up as most of us have been, into every corner of our minds."

—JOHN MAYNARD KEYNES (1883–1946), BRITISH ECONOMIST

America considers itself the land of new ideas, and in many respects it is. Yet the truth is that by the time we embrace them, so-called new ideas are usually anything but new. Most were hatched decades before being adopted. They had to travel a long and winding road, enduring repeated examination, debate—and rejection—before finally winning acceptance and bringing about real change.

The flat tax is no different. When I ran for president in 1996 and 2000, I proposed that today's monster federal income tax code be scrapped and replaced by a single tax rate for individuals and businesses.

The flat tax would do away with all but a few basic exemptions and deductions, eliminating the confusion and complexity of the current tax code and letting you fill out your return on a simple postcard or sheet of paper. A simple proposal, but one that promises, as you'll see in succeeding chapters, to transform not only the tax system but the nation as well, revitalizing the economy and changing our lives dramatically for the better.

Back then, this was portrayed as a new and radical idea. In fact, the flat tax has been around for decades. Some view it as a descendent of the "tithe" which exacted 10 percent off the fruits of men's labor in biblical times.

As you will see in later chapters of this book, our earliest system of income taxation was a flat tax. Lincoln enacted a 3 percent tax on income in 1861 to help finance the Civil War. The idea of graduated tax brackets was considered unfair and contrary to our traditions. Graduated brackets then came, but only briefly. The income tax itself was scrapped not long after the war.

By the mid-twentieth century, however, our view of taxation had changed. In the 1940s and 1950s, Americans had come to believe that, as a modern country, we needed to swallow the medicine of catastrophically high tax rates. Like castor oil, they were supposed to be good for us. In much the same way that Americans in the 1950s trusted that "Father Knows Best," the title of the classic television show of that era, we felt the government knew best about how to tax us and deploy our money.

But it doesn't. The federal tax code has grown into a 9-million-word, multi-headed hydra of countless brackets, deductions, and exemptions. Rates have come down significantly in the past 25 years. Yet when all of Washington's exactions—not just the income tax, but also Social Security and Medicare taxes and numerous excise taxes—are added together with state and local taxes, we annually surrender as much as 50 percent or more of our income to Uncle Sam and his equally voracious state and local kin.

Every April fifteenth—and for entrepreneurs, every quarter—we keep saying we've had enough. Like Howard Beale in the classic movie

"Network," we want to throw open the window and shout at the top of our lungs that we're mad as hell and not going to take it anymore.

But we don't. We may be incensed at tax time and consider the federal tax code an unfair, excessive burden. But most of us accept today's system as a fact of life, as immutable as lousy weather.

Until recently, few people have been bold enough to suggest that we don't have to take it, that the system can be changed—and that real change can work. But, as this book will show, reform is not only possible: It is essential—and inevitable.

The flat tax has already produced results around the world—from Russia to Hong Kong and elsewhere. As you'll see later in this book, it is part of a new worldwide wave of tax simplification that has implications for America's competitive position in the world economy. The flat tax movement is finally being recognized by media organizations that had once been skeptical, including the *Economist* magazine, which devoted an April 2005 cover story to the growing worldwide support for the flat tax.

America's relative lateness to the table is ironic when you consider that the first calls for a modern flat tax system in this country began in the 1960s when in their groundbreaking book, *Capitalism and Freedom* (1962), economists Milton and Rose Friedman proposed a "flat-rate tax."

The prime movers behind the flat tax movement in America have been Robert Hall and Alvin Rabushka, economists at the Hoover Institution. Their highly influential book, *The Flat Tax*, first appeared in the early 1980s and provided the impetus for a series of legislative proposals, the first serious attempts at reform.

Throughout the 1980s, the flat tax was periodically discussed. It emerged as a national issue for the first time when former California governor Jerry Brown, campaigning for the 1992 Democratic presidential nomination, called for a 13 percent flat tax on all personal and business income. His plan did away with the Social Security tax, retaining exemptions for mortgage interest, charitable contributions, and adding a new one—a deduction for rent. Along with the flat tax,

Brown proposed a Europe-like value added tax (VAT) of 13 percent. I loved Brown's idea of the flat tax, but realized that his VAT would lead us down a perilous path toward European economic stagnation. Nonetheless, his flat tax idea was breathtaking and groundbreaking.

Brown's flat tax proposal rightly got him plenty of attention—making him a serious contender against frontrunner Bill Clinton. Even the *New York Times* was favorable to the idea of a flat tax back then.

Brown was not the only Democrat to support what some see, incorrectly, as an exclusively Republican idea. Few may recall now that no less a Democrat than former House Minority Leader Richard Gephardt once pushed a variation of the flat tax idea, a stance from which he later retreated. Other flat tax plans have been floated by Republicans, including former House Majority Leader Dick Armey (R-TX).

I believe the stage is now set and that conditions are more conducive than ever to the introduction of a flat tax in this country. Our prior belief in a 1950s "government knows best" high-tax approach has been replaced by widespread recognition that a flat tax which combines stark simplicity with a tax cut, would generate *more*, not less, government revenue.

The salutary effects of tax reduction on the economy have been demonstrated. Starting with the Harding-Coolidge tax cuts in the 1920s and the Kennedy tax cuts in the early 1960s, we have seen how lower tax rates produce prosperity. (Amazing to think that the Democrats in the 1960s were the tax cutters and the Republicans thought such cuts were fiscally irresponsible, a total role reversal from today.) In the late 1970s, the Kemp-Roth tax cut proposal for an across-the-board 30 percent tax cut was adopted by Ronald Reagan when he became president and launched what became the then-longest economic boom in American history.

As our history chapter makes clear, Reagan's dramatic reforms were undone by subsequent administrations. Today President Bush is attempting to revive meaningful tax reform with his call in 2001 for elimination of the death tax, and two years later, a similar call for doing away with the dividend tax. He also ushered in a cut in the capital gains tax and allowed more expensing of investments for business. Yes, there have been roadblocks. The president's proposal for supersavings accounts was quickly dropped; the death tax expires in 2010 for just a year, to be reincarnated in 2011. And even the president's 2005 panel on tax reform, which was formed as I wrote this book, will base its recommendations on static analysis techniques (see chapter seven) believed by many experts to be highly inaccurate in predicting the impact of tax initiatives, especially tax cuts, on the economy.

And yet...the spirit of reform is in the air. The administration has proposed a host of free market initiatives—from taxes to tort reform to private Social Security accounts—that are causing us to reexamine how the government is structured and financed and how it provides services. At last many people are asking, just how much is the government entitled to take from what we earn? And how much is too much?

Meanwhile, ordinary citizens approach me at airports, TV studios, professional and social events, asking: *Do you think that we will ever see a flat tax?* There is a plaintive tone, a note of frustration in their voices. Small business people complain that, for all the smooth talk, the politicians don't get it. All they care about, they say, is finding excuses to increase government spending and get as much money as they can without losing their jobs. *They don't understand that every dollar they take is one that we need to pay our people and stay in business. They don't understand what we go through.*

That's why I wrote this book—to get beyond the sound bites, the political agendas that so often color day-to-day reporting and, instead, encourage a full and reasoned discussion of the issues during this critical period of national debate; to show in clear and compelling terms that the flat tax works. The evidence is there—in the historical facts, economic statistics, and the experiences of nations that have implemented a flat tax system.

The need for a flat tax could not be greater at a time when tax reform overseas is helping to produce new global competitors—countries in Asia and Central and Eastern Europe whose low tax policies have spawned a gold rush of foreign investment. Even high-tax nations in Europe with their stagnant economies have awakened to the threat of these emerging dynamos. America needs to respond.

The flat tax is a reform of our federal income tax system. It does not affect, for example, state and local taxes. But, contrary to what some may fear, it will generate *increased* government revenue. And that powerful example will induce, I believe, similar reforms in state and local taxes.

Another fact that people seldom realize: the increased revenues and increased value of the nation's assets that will result from the flat tax will certainly help us grapple with the fiscally challenged Social Security and Medicare programs.

America has a great future. The flat tax will help us achieve it.

CHAPTER ONE

Today's Federal Tax Code: Nightmare on Main Street

*"In this world nothing can be said to be certain,
except death and taxes."*

–BENJAMIN FRANKLIN

Benjamin Franklin's maxim about the inevitability of taxes is so familiar that it has the ring of a cliché. But it suggests a profound truth: Taxes are a certainty we dread almost as much as death. No matter what our politics may be, when tax time approaches we all do our best to pay as little as possible. Some people go so far as to avoid taxes altogether.

Taxes and tax law may seem like dry subjects, but they've incited passions from the beginning of time. Even the American Revolution, with its rallying cry of "No taxation without representation," had its roots in a quarrel over taxation. Years later, the Founding Fathers' need to repay the debts of that war resulted in an excise tax on whiskey, which sparked the "Whiskey Rebellion," crushed by George Washington in the backwoods of Pennsylvania.

In the next century, protectionist tariffs on imported goods perceived to favor the fast-industrializing North helped divide the nation before the Civil War.

In the late 1970s, a popular uprising in California against excessive taxation eventually led to Ronald Reagan's election as president.

We so detest taxation that some people will resort to truly desperate measures. Lady Godiva's famous ride was prompted by indignation over excessive taxes. Her nobleman husband agreed to honor her pleas for tax relief for her fellow citizens—but only if she rode naked through town. Her resulting one-woman protest made history, exposing the unfairness of taxes—and then some.

Today, hardly a day goes by when we don't read about someone going to jail for tax avoidance. A handful of Americans have even given up their citizenship and moved abroad. Most of us condemn these tax dodgers, but shouldn't the tax code get some of the blame?

Given America's history of tax-o-phobia, how in the world did we end up with what we have today: our horrifically heavy, appallingly complex, corruption-inducing tax code? A monster of a system that not only reaches deep into our pockets—but overreaches into our lives. It influences our behavior, distorts our economy, and—yes—ruins our quality of life as individuals and a society. If you think that's overstated, consider the experiences of unlucky taxpayers who ran afoul of the system. This story appeared in the April 13, 2005, edition of *USA Today*:

> Eric Delore of Alameda, Calif., owes the IRS more than $400,000. He didn't participate in a tax shelter or invent illegal deductions for a home-based business. Delore, a technology professional, is in debt because he received incentive stock options from his former employer. Those options pushed him into the nightmare world of the alternative minimum tax.

In 2000, Delore exercised stock options worth $1.1 million and held on to them so he could get a better tax rate when he sold. But his employer's stock price imploded when the tech bubble burst. By the time Delore sold his shares, they were worth $5,000. But because the AMT values stock options at the time of exercise, Delore was hit with a $420,000 tax bill.

There will be more on the Alternative Minimum Tax in subsequent chapters. Actually we think the name is a misnomer of Orwellian proportions—doublespeak for what really should be called the Alternative *Maximum* Tax, because the maximum is what you pay. Basically, the Alternative Minimum Tax is what you pay when Uncle Sam thinks you're able to take too many deductions. Sadly, AMT horror stories are all too common. As for Eric Delore, the married father of two, *USA Today* says that his struggles over the AMT have ruined him financially. "His bank accounts have been cleaned out and his paycheck intercepted. There's a lien on his house. He's tried twice to negotiate a lower tax bill with the IRS but was rejected both times." According to the paper, the ordeal may force him to file for bankruptcy protection.

Another AMT victim, Nina Doherty, worked for a small software company that gave her incentive stock options as part of her compensation. However she only got to exercise a portion of her stock options in 2000. Then the market fell and her stock value plummeted to virtually nothing.

But according to the IRS, she owed money to the government as a *prepayment* on future gains of the stock. While on a scouting trip with one of her daughters in 2001, her accountant called to inform her that her family's tax bill was essentially equal to their total annual income. Things went from bad to worse. The IRS seized $30,000 the family was planning to use for home repair and to buy a minivan. A lien was placed on their house and they were pushed to the verge of bankruptcy. In testimony last year before the Ways and Means Committee Oversight Subcommittee, Doherty blamed her tribulations on "the highly complex nature of the Alternative Minimum Tax [that] befuddled both my highly trained financial advisor and my accountant."

Such IRS abuses of taxpayer rights have been sufficient to warrant congressional hearings several years ago that led to a series of major reforms. Most of us don't get ensnared in the agency's toxic web. But even for the average taxpayer, the system is riddled with injustices. We all know the complaints:

FIRST AND FOREMOST, WE PAY TOO MUCH

And more than you'd think. Most Americans don't realize how far the politicians reach into our pockets. Everything we do is hit with some sort of tax, fee, or toll.

Consider an average day. You get up in the morning and turn on the light: you're socked with an array of electricity taxes. Turn on the water. Utility taxes. Put the coffee on. You probably paid sales tax on the coffee. Ditto any food you might eat.

Drive to work and you pay gasoline taxes and maybe a toll or two. You already paid fees on your license and registration. Not to mention the sales taxes you paid when buying the car, along with transfer fees and various add-ons local pols devised.

You get to work—and politicians take gargantuan bites out of your pay: Federal income taxes, state income taxes, Social Security taxes, Medicare taxes, and perhaps a local income tax.

Anything you buy or eat during the day has also been subjected to taxes. This doesn't mean that you pay all of them directly. When you buy, say, a new sweater, you're paying countless disguised taxes. These include the taxes that companies pay on their profits, along with workers' social security taxes, property taxes, utility taxes, corporate excise taxes, and more—all passed along to you in the form of higher prices.

But wait, your day isn't over. You go home, and, after more of those gas levies and tolls, you go through the mail. Uh oh, your county or township has sent your property taxes. Have a pet? Probably time to renew the license on Fido. Maybe you're thinking about getting married. Politicians say they love families, but they're going to charge you a fee to get hitched.

So what's the total tab? Politicians and many economists insist that "only" about one-third of our "economic output"—i.e., what we the people produce in goods and services each year—goes for taxes. But actually, when you get away from their weasel definitions of what constitutes a tax, you probably pay something like half of your income—or more.

Feel like calling Uncle Sam to complain? Watch out. You're paying taxes on that phone call—including an excise tax of currently 3 percent passed as a temporary financing measure to pay for the 1898 Spanish American War!

The politicians have anesthetized us to the scale of their tax larceny. Did We the People really give them the mandate to empty our wallets like this?

TAXES ARE TOO DAMN COMPLEX, ESPECIALLY THE FEDERAL INCOME TAX CODE

Consider this, for starters: Abraham Lincoln's Gettysburg Address, which defined the character of the nation, is all of 268 words. The Declaration of Independence runs about 1,300 words. The Constitution, which has served us for more than 2 centuries, comes to some 5,000 words. The Holy Bible has 773,000 words. The federal income tax code and all of its attendant rules and regulations: 9 *million* words and rising.

An appalling fact about the tax code is that *no one* really knows what's in it. That's why there are endless court cases over what our system actually allows and doesn't allow. And it's why there is so much ambiguity and confusion, why so many people and small businesses miss out on taking lawful deductions or end up making mistakes. It's why people with similar salaries can end up paying wildly different amounts of tax to Uncle Sam.

Indeed, how could anyone possibly know what's in the code when it reads like the following passage from the 2004 American Job Creation Act. And we quote:

Sec199(c) Special rule relating to election to treat cutting of timber as a sale or exchange.—

Any election under section 631(a) of the Internal Revenue Code of 1986 made for a taxable year ending on or before the date of the enactment of this Act may be revoked by the taxpayer for any taxable year ending after such date. For purposes of determining whether such taxpayer may make a further election under such section, such election (and any revocation under this section) shall not be taken into account. (p. 23)

Uh, run that by us again.

For those not fluent in taxcode-ese, the passage is explaining how cutting timber fits into the scheme of the new deduction for income from domestic manufacturing. If an owner of timber decides to cut and sell some trees, he can "revoke" his decision to file as having sold these trees for a gain under the new rules passed by Congress in October 2004.

We'll take their word for it. Here's another example, an excerpt from Section 274 (n) (2), titled "Exceptions to meals not allowed" as deductions under the code. Are you ready?

Sec 274 (n)(2) Exceptions to meals not allowed:

Paragraph (1) shall not apply to any expense if—

.... (E) such expense is for food or beverages—
    (i)   required by any Federal law to be provided to crew members of a commercial vessel,
    (ii) provided to crew members of a commercial vessel—
        (I)   which is operating on the Great Lakes, the Saint Lawrence Seaway, or any inland waterway of the United States, and
        (II) which is of a kind which would be required by Federal law to provide food and beverages to crew members if it were operated at sea,
    (iii) provided on an oil or gas platform or drilling rig if the platform or rig is located offshore, or

(iv) provided on an oil or gas platform or drilling rig, or at a support camp which is in proximity and integral to such platform or rig, if the platform or rig is located in the United States north of 54 degrees north latitude. Clauses (i) and (ii) of subparagraph (E) shall not apply to vessels primarily engaged in providing luxury water transportation (determined under the principles of subsection (m)). In the case of the employee, the exception of subparagraph (A) shall not apply to expenses described in subparagraph (D).

That's right, you deserve to deduct the full value of your meals if they're served on oil-rigs in Alaska located above fifty-four degrees north latitude. This passage may be more comprehensible than the first. Given its absurdity, we might have been better off if we hadn't understood it.

Little wonder that experts deciphering the code's perplexing prose are regularly flummoxed, as was powerfully illustrated in 1997 by a *Money* magazine survey. The editors gave 45 expert tax preparers a return to fill out on behalf of a fictional family, "the Bakers." What did they owe Uncle Sam? The experts came up with forty-five different answers! Not one came up with the right answer—or at least what *Money* thought was the right answer. Differences in their calculations ranged from a few hundred dollars to over $50,000.

At least that confusion was make-believe. Most of the time it is all too real.

Even the government's own tax pros don't understand the system. A 2003 Treasury Department study found that IRS experts manning the agency's toll-free help lines gave the wrong answers to tax-related questions more than 25 percent of the time. And yes, you are still liable for any errors, even if it's the IRS that makes the mistake!

Then there are those tax issues that are more exasperating—and inane—than the most arcane questions of medieval theology. Back then, they used to debate how many angels can dance on the head of a pin. Today's equivalent: How should trees be treated for tax purposes? Trees take decades to grow, which make them very different from cars.

An auto today can be manufactured in sixteen to twenty hours. Therefore, shouldn't the sale of trees be treated as capital gains?

Do you really want to know the answer? Amazingly, countless treatises and legal briefs have been written by lawyers and academics debating what the proper tax status of trees should be! Ready to throw your hands up in despair? You're not alone.

TAXES BREED CORRUPTION

America's federal income tax code is the chief political contaminant inside our nation's capital, encouraging the crassest, crudest political conduct.

Consider this: Fully one in six private-sector employees in Washington, D.C., is employed by the lobbying industry. Half of their efforts are directed at wrangling changes in the tax code. Each congressional term, endless interest groups and well-connected individuals push amendments with lucrative tax breaks favoring specific industries, companies—or themselves.

Many of these petitioners seek tax changes ostensibly designed to improve our lives. Shouldn't we help encourage homeownership? Institute a mortgage-interest deduction. Shouldn't we help people adopt children? Give them a tax credit of up to $10,390 for expenses paid to adopt a child under 18. Shouldn't we help reduce the marriage penalty? More credits and bigger exemptions for married couples.

As appealing and well-intentioned as they appear to be, such popular tax breaks, including the mortgage deduction, are too often a cover for myriad payoffs to politically potent special interests. Besides, if tax rates were low and reasonable in the first place, would we need all these credits? The answer for most deductions, exemptions, credits, deferrals, et cetera is an emphatic "No."

The tax code's ambiguity and incomprehensibility invite abuses. Too often, tax breaks benefit the few at the expense of the many. For example, during the 1990s, complicated corporate tax shelters proliferated. Their sole purpose was to cut companies' tax payments to Washington.

Most pretended to be legitimate business devices even though no real business purpose was served.

To see how the process of tax legislation has become a feeding frenzy, consider the American Jobs Creation Act that came before Congress last year. What started out as an attempt to abolish a paltry $5 billion a year export subsidy turned into "the most important tax bill in the last 20 years." It included about $140 billion of tax breaks. Our representatives somehow managed to find room for a $519 million tax break for small aircraft producers, a $44 million handout for importers of foreign-made ceiling fans and an $8 million loophole for bow and arrow makers (the Defense Department is looking to transform the military, after all). Starbucks (yes, Starbucks) notoriously had itself proclaimed a manufacturer and thus also qualified for a lower corporate tax rate.

After each round of new tax legislation, there is always strutting and breast-beating by lobbyists for those industries getting the most breaks. Publications routinely run lists of those who won and lost in each particular tax bill.

Ultimately the public is the loser. The *Long Island Business News* most aptly summed up the entire exercise: "American Jobs Creation Act: a 650-page boondoggle."

Too many tax code amendments and laws are the product of—and the excuse for—the exercise of raw political power. Politicians gladly rake in contributions—a form of extortion or protection buying—from groups or people wanting changes in the code.

You don't pay, you don't play. But if you pay, life can be very sweet indeed. For instance, ever wonder how the sugar lobby became so powerful? Sugar refiners and growers gave $2.4 million to Congress in 2004, more than any other agriculture group.[1] Their clout has given us a U.S. sugar program that keeps prices artificially high. As a result, Americans pay three times more for sugar than the rest of the world.

The rail industry, meanwhile, contributed $4.7 million last year to key representatives. The result? Amtrak receives an annual $1.2 billion subsidy to maintain many unprofitable rail routes throughout the country.

Astonishingly, members of Congress's House, Ways & Means Committee, which originates our tax legislation, usually rake in more contributions each election cycle than do most of their peers. Perhaps surprisingly, Ways and Means Committee members usually get more than even their colleagues on the House Appropriations Committee, which decides how and where your tax dollars are actually spent.

No wonder congressmen and congresswomen fight fiercely to be on that committee—you're set for political life if you are. Lobbyists, trade groups, and individuals will shower you with money in hopes of "gaining access" when new tax laws are written, which happens just about every year.

Chief Justice John Marshall once famously said, "The power to tax is the power to destroy." He also might have added, "And the power to reward favored interests."

Think of it this way: Washington politicians take one dollar from your pocket—and then return fifty cents in various tax deductions. Wouldn't it be better if they taxed you only that fifty cents in the first place?

We would be better off—we'd keep more of what we earned—with a simple, flat tax.

TAXES ARE UNFAIR

Thanks to all those tax breaks, people with similar incomes often end up with vastly different tax liabilities. An example of this is provided, once more, by that demon offspring of the tax beast, the AMT, or Alternative Minimum Tax. As the *New York Times* reported in February 2005, "People in towns with high property taxes sometimes face the AMT, while others with similar incomes in the next town do not...Consider a married couple with three children, living in Massachusetts and making $100,000 a year. With a typical size home equity loan and $9,000 in property taxes, the couple could face an AMT surcharge of almost $700, increasing their federal tax bill to nearly $11,000 from $10,300, according to Ernst & Young. A similar couple paying significantly less in property taxes would not fall under the alternative tax."

Even tax breaks designed to improve our lives usually lead to unfairness. Take, for instance, the tax credit for buyers of certain hybrid cars. Its intent is to encourage fuel efficiency and concern about the environment. But why shouldn't low-income people get a tax break when buying an ordinary vehicle—one that is probably a greater financial burden for them?

And what about the people who live in Texas, New Hampshire, and other states with no state income tax? Unlike citizens in higher tax states, they can't deduct that state income tax from their federal income tax bill. In effect, Uncle Sam is subsidizing states that tax their citizens.

Then there are the businesses that get tax deductions for paying for employees' health insurance. But the secretary who works for a company without such a plan and wants to buy one for herself and her family isn't so lucky. Sorry Mom, you must pay for your insurance with after-tax dollars. What's the justice of that?

And remember the recent legislation that deemed Starbucks a "manufacturer" worthy of tax breaks? How did that happen? The company's well-paid lobbyists convinced the government—with a straight face—that grinding coffee beans is a form of manufacturing. Now could you imagine what the IRS would do if *you* claimed a tax deduction for grinding coffee in your kitchen? And on it goes.

Then there's the absurdity—and, as you've seen, the abuses—of the Alternative Minimum Tax (AMT). Congress gives you deductions but woe to the taxpayer who tries to take all of them. The AMT was originally designed to make sure the ultra rich didn't escape taxation. Now it ensnares ever millions more middle income tax payers each year. For example, a family with 6 children and an income of $92,000 taking the standard deduction would be hit with another $900 in income taxes.

TAXES ARE JOB KILLERS

That's self-evident. When the politicians over-tax, you have less money to buy goods and services, grow a business, and hire people—less money to fuel our overall economic growth.

The idea is simple: When you lower the price of things, you generally get more of them. Raise the price and you reduce demand—and supply. Taxes are the "price" the government charges us to work, take risks, and run businesses that create jobs. Higher taxes penalize people for such productive activities. As a result, they kill jobs.

The classic example: The devastating Great Depression that ensued after the Smoot-Hawley tariff slapped oppressive taxes on hundreds of imports. Other countries retaliated. A trade war erupted. Products became unaffordable and people bought less. As a result manufacturers had to cut back employment. A deadly downward spiral ensued. Profits shriveled and investment capital dried up, undermining banks and thereby deepening the economic slump.

The Great Depression was made even worse in the U.S. by massive tax increases that were enacted in 1932 in the name of balancing the budget. Those horrific increases crushed an already enfeebled economy. Had there been no Great Depression, Hitler would never have come to power. Imagine how different the decade of the 1930s would have been if the U.S. had had a strong, vibrant, confident economy.

We saw the destructive side of taxes again in the 1970s. Inflation pushed people into higher tax brackets. Congress made matters infinitely worse by, among other things, substantially boosting the capital gains tax. The result was, again, predictable. Would-be new ventures couldn't get financing. Productivity fell. A family making $18,000 a year in 1979 was less well off than a family that had made $7,000 in 1968. Jimmy Carter called it all a national malaise.

And remember what happened in 1990 when Washington politicians—ever hungry for more of your money—enacted something called the luxury tax? Boat buyers had to pay an extra 10 percent on the price of a "luxury" vessel. Car buyers got hit with a ten percent tax on any so-called luxury vehicle whose price exceeded $30,000. Result? Suddenly consumers exhibited a keen interest in "pre-owned" automobiles. The boat building industry in Maine and elsewhere was devastated. Buyers balked at the higher prices. Instead of buying new, they bought used vessels on which there was no tax.

Fortunately, the tax was eventually phased out. But the fundamental lesson—that taxes can kill commerce—has been lost on politicians to this day.

We haven't even gotten to the other way taxes kill jobs—through compliance costs. Just ask a small business owner what he or she spends on accounting fees or legal fees.

In 2004, the Office of Management & Budget estimated that our nation's total compliance cost is some $200 billion. That includes accounting fees and expenses as well as the sheer number of hours spent accumulating the volumes of records and data—W-2s, 1099s, and the like—necessary to fill out your return. Compliance costs add up to the salary equivalent of at least 3 million jobs. All this is money that companies can't use to expand and innovate, dollars families can't use to pay off credit card bills or to finance their children's educations.

By hurting economic growth, the tax code prevents us from improving our standard of living and creating wealth. It punishes savings by taxing dividends two or more times. The 2003 tax bill ameliorated this somewhat by reducing the maximum dividend tax for individuals to 15 percent. But the rate should be zero; after all, companies have already paid taxes on that money.

Then there's the death tax, or the so-called estate tax, that destroys capital. Your estate is taxed on assets that were already taxed when you were alive—making it harder for you to provide for surviving family members.

High tax rates make it extremely difficult for most Americans to amass vital savings for college, retirement, or the starting of a business.

Congress has responded by creating a complex assortment of tax credits—401(K)s, 529s, IRAs, Roth IRAs, tax-deferred annuities, et cetera. They simply raise the question, "Why not make life simpler by slashing tax rates and letting us keep more of what we earn?"

For the answer, one need only look at what happens when the tax burden is lowered. People and businesses invest, innovate, and produce. When taxes have been dramatically cut, as happened in the 1960s and 1980s, the economy blossomed. Millions of new jobs were created. Government receipts went up.

Taxes enormously impact how much and how well we work. Why are we more productive than Europe? Because our tax burden is lower. Few recall now that, decades ago, when our tax burdens were similar, European workers worked just as hard as American workers. Today, Europe's high taxes have given countries such as France and Germany unemployment rates twice our own. Their rate of job creation is a fraction of ours.

By happy contrast, look at the 1980s. President Ronald Reagan slashed income taxes across the board. Critics howled that this was financially irresponsible. But Reagan knew what he was doing. When his cuts were fully phased in the economy took off like a rocket. Eighteen million new jobs were created. Silicon Valley blossomed. America became a font of innovation and invention. Federal government revenues doubled. The net wealth of the nation increased by seventeen trillion dollars, ten times the increase in the national debt.

Reagan's was no isolated example. We saw the same phenomenon in the 1920s and the 1960s, and not just in this country. Britain's Margaret Thatcher, prime minister from 1979 to 1990, took a meat ax to Britain's draconian taxes. Britain almost overnight changed economically from being Europe's sick man to having Europe's most vibrant large economy.

THE TAX CODE MAKES NO SENSE—FOR THE TAXPAYER OR SOCIETY

Not only does the tax code confound taxpayers with complexity. It also leads to a misallocation of resources that makes no economic sense.

Take the sad case of real estate, which I discuss in chapter three. Long story short: the industry got enormous tax breaks in 1981, which led to a fevered real estate investment boom. Money poured in, attracted not by demand but favorable tax treatment. Shopping centers and office buildings went up with no regard as to who might rent the space.

Only in the movies can you build a baseball field and expect they will come. In the real world, the customers may not. Empty office buildings pock-marked many American cities. Hotels in Texas often had no guests. Developers were so desperate to unload their properties that the joke in Texas was that when you paid a hotel bill, you needed to make sure they hadn't slipped in the hotel itself.

The awful consequences of this overbuilding were made worse when, in 1986, many of the shelters were abruptly removed. Real estate prices crashed, helping to precipitate the savings and loan bank crisis. S&Ls had been heavy lenders to real estate speculators. Thousands of S&Ls went under, costing taxpayers over $90 billion.

Later I discuss how corporate tax deductions with the noble intention of helping people get health insurance have had the unintended, perverse consequence of leaving millions of Americans uninsured, along with fueling out-of-control inflation in our health care costs.

Then there are those economically useless, abusive tax shelters. Companies and accountants wrack their brains figuring ways to cut taxes through exotic maneuvers that don't really produce genuinely needed products and services. The Government Accountability Office of the U.S. government released a report noting that since 1993 the government has lost $85 billion in tax payments to such convoluted tax strategies.[2]

What to do about these outrages? Simple. As a free people, we must cry, "Enough!" We need a new tax system that is simple, honest, and fair. This book proposes that we start with the Federal tax code, the biggest, most corrosive component of our tax system.

There is only one way to deal with this abomination: get rid of it. Start over. Return to fundamental American principles of clarity and common sense.

This is why we should demand a flat tax. There would be one rate—17 percent—after generous exemptions for adults and children. Under the flat tax, for example, a family of four would pay no federal income tax on its first $46,165 of income and would pay only 17 cents on every dollar it earned above that level.

THE FLAT TAX WILL ELIMINATE THE OUTRAGES AND INJUSTICES

No more fear and loathing as April 15 approaches. No more worrying over whether you have all your necessary records. No more complications—you could literally fill out your tax form on a single page or even a postcard.

The flat tax will put an end to ambiguity. No more mind-numbing, tension-filled hours of trying to gather together all your records. No more wondering what's kosher on your tax return and what isn't.

But a flat tax will do more than make figuring out your income-tax liability a simple task. It will unleash the full economic potential of our country, igniting growth in the form of more jobs and innovation, more government revenue and dollars to fund programs like Social Security and Medicare. Utilizing sophisticated economic modeling that takes into account the real world context of tax changes, Fiscal Associates has determined that, over the course of ten years, the flat tax will create some $6 trillion in new assets and $892 billion in additional payroll tax receipts.

The flat tax will remove a principle source of political corruption in Washington—special interests getting special tax breaks at your expense. No more opportunities for abuses.

And to make sure the Washington politicians don't quickly revert to their old, bad habits, the flat tax will have a supermajority provision: Taxes could only be raised by a 60 percent vote by Congress, instead of a simple majority.

Is this too good to be true? When I proposed the flat tax during my run for president in 1996 and again in 2000, the naysayers reacted with blistering criticisms. They insisted that it would favor the rich, hurt the poor, destroy home ownership, wreck charities—just about everything except provoke a plague of locusts.

The governor of New Hampshire, who supported one of my opponents in 1996, went on TV to warn that my plan would bankrupt his state's homeowners. He conveniently "forgot" that, under my original plan, a family of four would pay no federal income tax on their first $36,000 of income. He wrongly applied the 17 percent rate to that $36,000, thereby adding about $6,000 to that family's tax bill. Needless to say, he never acknowledged this crucial omission.

Not surprisingly, H&R Block, the country's largest preparer of individual income tax returns, also voiced "concerns" over the flat tax. During the 1996 campaign, they sent a mailing to New Hampshire voters with the dire prediction that the flat tax would hurt middle class Americans by eliminating popular deductions, such as for home mortgages, and virtually destroy civilization as we know it. The fact that my flat tax would give everyone a tax cut was conveniently overlooked.

Of course, the only ones the flat tax will hurt are those like H&R Block and others who live off our tangled tax code. Who would need a tax preparer if you could fill out your tax return on a postcard or simple sheet of paper? With a straight face, H&R Block executives insisted that their position had nothing to do with the fact that the flat tax would essentially put them out of business!

Even Fannie Mae, the nation's largest buyer of home mortgages, opposed the flat tax, playing on fears of what it would do to homeowners. However, as I explain in chapter seven, the flat tax will actually reduce interest rates, including mortgage rates. It will increase the value of housing and leave homeowners with more after-tax income. But these truths escaped their notice. Unfortunately, Fannie reported "the facts" about the flat tax about as carefully as they've handled their accounting.

Meanwhile, other naysayers, supposed champions of the underprivileged, asserted that the flat tax would hurt the poor. They ignored the fact that, at that time, the flat tax would have resulted in massive tax relief for twenty million low-income earners, effectively removing them from the federal income tax rolls. Why they believed that struggling wage earners would be hurt by being allowed to keep more of what they earn was never really explained.

Equally unfounded are concerns over the impact of a flat tax on charitable giving. Americans don't need to be bribed by the tax code to give. As I lay out in chapter seven in detail, history demonstrates that people give whether income tax rates are high or low. The bottom line:

when the American people have more, they give more. With the flat tax, they would keep more and earn more. Yet many philanthropic organizations attacked the flat tax.

Such "misconceptions," combined with the wariness of human nature, made it difficult for some people to see that the flat tax is a tax cut. They focused instead on what they would lose. That's why I've proposed taxpayers be given a choice: They could go with the new flat tax or they can stay with the old tax system. Don't take my word for it. Decide for yourself which is better for you. Most people with common sense will quickly see that new is better.

They'll disregard the naysayers and their self-interested rhetoric and know the truth: The flat tax will work.

It already does work. As I'll show in chapter six, in the growing number of countries where a flat tax has been adopted, results have been astonishing. Once depressed economies of nations such as Latvia, Lithuania, Estonia, Russia, and elsewhere are blossoming. Government revenues are booming. Hong Kong has had a variant of the flat tax for almost sixty years that has helped transform the region into one of the world's most prosperous.

Hardly a month goes by without another country announcing that it is instituting a flat tax. Amazingly, the idea is beginning to take hold in "old Europe"—where a growing number of German experts are advocating the system.

So impressive are these flat tax success stories that *The Economist*, which treated the flat tax idea with frosty skepticism when I ran, recently reversed course with a dramatic cover story boldly endorsing the flat tax. The magazine asked, "In Britain, tax simplification is nowhere on the agenda. Why not?" Last year Chinese financial authorities brought over one of the original flat tax architects, Alvin Rabushka, co-author of the seminal book, *The Flat Tax*, to draw from his expertise on how one might be adopted.

What are we waiting for? That's why I wrote this book. The rest of the world is not staying still. China and India, with their mammoth economies, are determined to catch up with us. A growing number of

European countries are seeing the flat tax as a way to leap ahead in an ever more competitive world.

That's why the need to rethink our tax system is more critical than ever. This book reveals the reality of the flat tax—what it is, why it works, and, most of all, why adopting one is so important to the future of this country. We go beyond the sound bites that you've heard, with facts and figures that do not merely belie the naysayers, but show them to be 100 percent, absolutely and fundamentally *wrong!*

The flat tax will make us more prosperous. It will reduce political pollution and corruption. It will be fair and transparent—the Enrons of the world will find it harder to play their games if our fetid tax swamp were drained. It will restore America's faith in our lawmaking. It will make us more competitive overseas. It will give rise to a strong, innovative, and dynamic economy that will help us wage a successful war against Islamic terrorism.

The flat tax will deal a devastating blow to a Washington political culture more interested in special interests than in the well being of America.

CHAPTER TWO

How It Began: The Birth of the Tax Beast

"Would it not be better to simplify the system of taxation rather than to spread it over such a variety of subjects and pass through so many new hands."

—THOMAS JEFFERSON, 1784

How did we, as freedom-loving Americans, end up with the beast that is our present tax code? Our current system is widely accepted today as a fact of life. Yet it is a huge break from our traditions and far from what was intended in the early days of the republic. Our nation was founded, as every schoolchild knows, as a consequence of our aversion to "taxation without representation." The North American colonies rose up in rebellion, after Britain imposed a raft of new taxes—including the much despised Stamp Tax, which required that stamps, for a fee, be put on most legal and commercial papers and documents[1] to defray the expense of defending the newly expanded North American frontiers and the broader British empire. After winning the fight for self-determination, the Founding Fathers sought to establish a nation whose citizens were free to enjoy the fruits of their labors, unimpeded by a tax-hungry government. No less a figure than Thomas Jefferson wrote that excessive taxation was in direct opposition to this ideal.

In fact, Jefferson's writings on taxation favor the concept of a simple system based on a single tax. "Having already paid its tax as Income, to pay another tax on the thing it purchased, is paying twice for the same thing; it is an aggrievance on the citizen...[and] contrary to the most sacred of the duties of a government," he wrote in 1816.

Alexander Hamilton, our first secretary of the treasury, discouraged the idea of an income tax. He asserted in the Federalist Papers, "It is evident from the state of the country, from the habits of the people, from the experience we have had on the point itself, that it is impracticable to raise any very considerable sums by direct taxation."

Hamilton backed the dollar with gold, consolidated debt, instituted a simple system of taxation and allowed government bonds to be used as currency to pay taxes. His initiatives produced a steady stream of revenue that propelled the nation to solvency and bolstered the economy—all the while maintaining relatively low taxes.

Imagine what Hamilton and Jefferson would think of today's mammoth tax code, with its multiple rates and convoluted system of deductions! In our earliest days, America had no income tax. The biggest source of tax revenue was tariffs on imported goods. There were also internal levies on a variety of items, including whiskey.

Not only were our taxes light back then, but any attempt to raise them was met with fierce opposition from our independent-minded citizens. The whiskey tax, for example, provoked a furious uprising in the backwoods of Pennsylvania. Tax collectors were run out of town—that is, if they were lucky. The unlucky ones were tarred and feathered. Washington had to raise an army and respond by force. The rebellion was eventually put down. The episode played a critical role in shaping America's view of how the tax system was supposed to work. We believed that taxes should be minimal. They should be imposed by the representatives of the people. Yet once levied, they had to be paid—or else.

Ferocious disputes, however, continued over import tariffs. To help protect its emerging industries, the North favored high tariffs; the agricultural South, more dependent on imports, opposed them. The so-called Tariff of Abominations—which substantially raised duties on both manufactured goods and raw materials—was passed in 1828 and further polarized the North and South, precipitating a national crisis. Southerners felt the tariff would not only raise prices on necessary goods but might also reduce British exports to the U.S., thereby making it harder for the British to pay for Southern cotton.

Siding with his fellow Southerners, Vice President John Calhoun of South Carolina made history by defiantly opposing his own boss, President Andrew Jackson. Calhoun asserted that states could declare the tariff—or any federal law—null and void, the so-called Doctrine of Nullification. President Jackson furiously responded that he would personally hang his vice president from a lamppost if Calhoun followed through on his threat to have the South Carolina militia forcibly obstruct enforcement of the tariff or any other federal law that Calhoun's state didn't cotton to. Fortunately, in the face of Jackson's implacable opposition, Calhoun and South Carolina rescinded their Ordinance of Nullification, when given a face-saving nominal cut in tariff duties.

The only other times the government tried to impose new taxes was in times of war, such as during the War of 1812 against the British. By taxing land, slaves, and estates and by raising tariffs, the federal government was able to collect the money to meet its military challenges. It may be hard to believe today, but between 1817 and the start of the Civil War in 1861, the federal government operated successfully without having to levy any new internal taxes. In fact, Andrew Jackson eliminated the national debt during his presidency by deftly managing existing revenues and through the sale of federal lands.

The onset of the Civil War, though, marked a milestone in the history of American taxation. Insatiable demands for money to fund that conflict forced the federal government in 1861 to enact a first-ever federal income tax. Slowly, the tax beast, as we know it today, began to rear its ugly head. Of course the beast was a lot smaller back then: The government started out by imposing just a 3 percent tax on all incomes higher than $800.

Politicians at the time heatedly and prophetically debated whether there should be a single, flat rate or a graduated rate system. In 1862, the forces of complexity won out, resulting in a simple version of a graduated system: 3 percent on incomes more than $600 up to $10,000; any incomes higher were taxed at 5 percent. There were exemptions for rental housing, repairs, losses, and other taxes paid. In 1864 rates were raised again and still more layers were added: 5 percent on incomes up to $5,000; 7.5 percent on incomes between $5,000; and $10,000 and 10 percent on incomes above $10,000. The monster as we know it was born.

The income tax was a dramatic departure. But tax-loathing Americans were still not ready to make it permanent. The Civil War ended and the tax was subsequently repealed. For the moment, the tax monster was defeated. But Pandora's box had been opened. Over the next century, Americans would be gradually lured back into the beast's embrace. Twenty years later, the monster's minions tried again. The federal government enacted an income tax in 1894. As Peter Dobkin Hall of Harvard's Kennedy School of Government recounts in the April 15, 2005, edition of the *New York Times*: "By the early 1890s, the annual incomes of tycoons like John D. Rockefeller and Andrew Carnegie were greater than the tax revenues of most states. Concerned about the implications of such a concentration of wealth...Congress enacted a federal income tax..."

Almost immediately, writes Dobkin, the complexity and confusion began: "The income tax legislation left many questions unanswered. A single page of small print summarized 'instructions relative to annual returns'..." Dobkin writes that, although "the full legislation and accompanying regulations totaled a mere forty pages." That's brief by today's standards—but far from clear. Rockefeller's attorneys had to submit questions on everything from "what kinds of income needed to be declared" to "how to treat depreciation of assets and investment losses."

When the new income tax was announced, Rockefeller had considered not filing a return at all. His lawyers persuaded him to do so. Otherwise, they said, the government "'will assess Mr. Rockefeller at some outrageous figure and add the penalties.' By filing his own return, they concluded, Rockefeller's payment, 'would be far less than anything they would put down.'" Some things, alas, never change.

Rockefeller filed his return—he paid a 2 percent tax totaling $14,961—in 1895. But he and others were later granted a reprieve. The Supreme Court declared that law unconstitutional a year later.

Yet pressure for a national income tax persisted. Tariffs, which raised the cost of essential goods, were depicted as unfair to working people. And the still-agrarian South continued to oppose them.

In 1909, President William Howard Taft's successful enactment of a corporate income tax laid the groundwork for acceptance of the idea of a personal income tax—allowing the beast to rise again. Four years later, in 1913, the Sixteenth Amendment to the Constitution was finally ratified, and a personal income tax was imposed.

Congress passed a progressive income tax beginning at 1 percent and moving up to 7 percent for those having incomes of more than $500,000 (the equivalent today of about $15 million in income).

So the tax monster made a comeback—though fortunately it was still lot smaller than what we know today. As a result of the new law, only 4 people out of 1,000 paid income tax—in contrast to the more than 130 million who now file individual tax returns.

But, being voracious, the beast swiftly grew. The simple, low-rate tax system became a victim of the First World War. Our entry into the war in 1917 sent levies rocketing upward. Tax revenues collected by the federal government were soon nearly equal to all collections for the previous 125 years combined.

Before the war was over, the top tax rate had risen from 7 percent to an astounding 77 percent. World War I not only saw the growth of the beast but also an unprecedented accumulation of power by the federal government. To help mobilize for the war effort, Washington seized railroads, as well as the telephone and telegraph industries. War boards were established that gave Washington huge powers over the private sector—allocating raw materials, setting prices and wages, closing and opening plants, and controlling the prices, production, and distribution of food—all in the name of boosting wartime production. This immense power was intoxicating to those who worked in and around government, including Assistant Secretary of the Navy Franklin D. Roosevelt. Not surprisingly, Roosevelt and others were entranced by the notion of the supposedly great things that could be achieved in peacetime by a federal government whose powers were expanded as in war.

Fortunately, America's low-tax tradition kept these fantasies in check—at least for a while. During the 1920s, income taxes were cut across the board; the top rate was slashed from 77 percent to 25 percent. The national debt was reduced by a third. America boomed. The 1920s was a decade of fantastic innovation. Movies, radios, automobiles, and numerous new household appliances, such as refrigerators and washing machines, became affordable for millions of middle-class Americans. The U.S. underwent the world's greatest road-building program since the days of the Roman Empire. Then came the Great Depression, the most devastating smash-up the American economy—and the world—had ever experienced. Millions of jobs were rapidly destroyed. Millions of farmers lost their land.

American incomes precipitously shrank—drastically reducing living standards for even those who still had jobs. Thousands of banks went bust, which wiped out the savings that could have helped countless people better absorb the hammering blows these desolate times dealt them.

The key cause of this catastrophe was the Smoot-Hawley tariff, which imposed extremely high taxes on countless imports.[2] European nations retaliated by taxing or banning U.S. goods and a disastrous trade war resulted that killed world commerce and caused the economic collapse.

But the politicians didn't get it. Despite the role of taxes in triggering the crisis, President Hoover sought in 1932 to "restore confidence" by balancing the budget through—that's right—a massive, calamitous increase in taxes. The top income tax rate was boosted from 25 percent to 63 percent. Hoover's tax hikes only made the economy worse, sending unemployment from 15 percent to 25 percent, almost five times today's level.

The Depression would have been far less harsh and the recovery far quicker had Hoover lived up to his historical image as a do-nothing chief executive. In reality, he was a big-government activist, and his activism in instituting higher taxes did immensely more harm than good.

His successor, the buoyant, extremely confident Franklin Roosevelt, dramatically, excitingly revived the morale of the nation. But again, contrary to many historians' perceptions, his economic policies were mostly counterproductive. FDR raised taxes even more. He imposed a breathless array of new, anti-business regulations. For the first time in American history, an economic recovery did not exceed the peak of the previous expansion. Early in his second term, Roosevelt presided over another sickening economic slide. America didn't truly recover from the Great Depression until the advent of the Second World War.

With America's entry into World War II after Japan's attack on Pearl Harbor on December 7, 1941, taxes were expanded as never before. Personal income tax rates rose to 23 percent for those in the lowest bracket and to 94 percent for those with incomes over $1 million.

What a change from the 1 percent to 7 percent brackets of the original 1913 income tax! The tax beast was here to stay. Americans, for the most part, accepted it as the price a free people must pay to preserve freedom and defeat a monstrous, murderous tyranny. When the war was won, however, income tax rates were not brought down the way they had been after World War I. The subsequent Cold War and the three-year Korean War kept rates high. Political leaders didn't understand in those days that punitive rates hurt economic growth. They failed to comprehend that reducing high tax levels would have actually enabled the economy to get stronger, generating more revenue for the government.

World War II also ushered in a new era of tax collection, changing forever the way Americans pay Uncle Sam. Until the war, we paid our income taxes in a single lump sum each year. But now, thanks to higher tax rates, millions of people for the first time couldn't save enough money to pay the larger amounts they owed the Bureau of Internal Revenue, as the IRS was then called.

What to do? Washington realized it could not jail millions of non-complying Americans. And so it invented withholding. Like department store customers paying for consumer goods on an installment plan, people would pay a part of their tax bill with each paycheck. Voila, thought the bureaucrats, your problems were solved. Taxpayers using withholding wouldn't be walloped by a mammoth bill each year. Your employer would gradually deduct from your paycheck what you owe over twelve months. You'd never even have to see that money! Uh, gee thanks.

The problem with withholding is that it reduces the discomfort of paying income tax by spreading payments out over the course of a year. Americans end up feeling a sting instead of a painful bite. Withholding made collection easier. But it also made Americans less acutely aware of the impact of taxes on their financial well-being—allowing the system to grow more easily and become less accountable. And, like income taxes themselves, withholding was supposed to be a temporary wartime measure!

Tax rates were reduced somewhat after World War II, but were again boosted at the onset of the Korean War. President Dwight D. Eisenhower ended the Korean conflict in 1953, but in the name of balancing the budget, he refused to support any major tax reductions—thereby helping to give us recessions in 1954, 1958, and 1960.

America's fabled prosperity of the 1950s was not nearly as vigorous as it would have been had the tax system been more benign. As incomes rose, more and more people found themselves in chokingly high tax brackets. Tax shelters, especially in commercial real estate, became more common. The U.S. economy grew more sluggish as the 1950s wore on.

Finally, in the early 1960s, President John F. Kennedy proposed dramatic tax cuts as a spur to growth. These reductions were enacted by President Lyndon Johnson after Kennedy's assassination. The highest tax bracket was whacked from 91 percent to 70 percent; the lowest bracket, from 20 percent to 14 percent. The U.S. economy boomed. Washington's revenues blossomed. Receipts from the highest income earners almost doubled within three years. Then came the Vietnam War and with it a 10 percent income tax surcharge, imposed in 1967. The highest rate went from 70 percent to 77 percent.

Relief was supposed to come when this top rate on salaries and wages, so-called earned income, was reduced to 50 percent in 1969 (The highest rate on dividends and interest, though, was 70 percent). However, at the same time, the capital gains tax was catastrophically raised, which more than undid the benefits of this reduction. The high capital gains levy punished individuals and companies for taking risks. Investors aren't going to risk money on unproven ventures if the rewards are overly taxed. As a result, the stock market stagnated. The American economy turned sluggish. Then as the 1970s progressed, things got worse. Congress raised the maximum capital gains tax even higher, to almost 50 percent. Inflation kicked people into higher tax brackets—remember, a family earning $7,000 in 1968 was better off than a family earning $18,000 in 1979.

Something dramatic had to be done. In 1980, Ronald Reagan took office after defeating President Jimmy Carter. Reagan sat at the helm of a nation with disastrously high taxes, economic stagnation, a severely depressed stock market, and out-of-control inflation. America was reeling from setbacks overseas, thanks to Carter's gutting the military and his weak, dithering foreign policy.

Reagan slashed income tax rates, reined in non-military government spending and pushed economic deregulation. He also launched a massive military build-up and instituted a confident, assertive foreign policy to challenge the Soviet Union. Reagan's approach on taxes had already been vindicated in 1978, when Congress, against the wishes of President Carter, cut the maximum capital gains tax from a suffocating level of nearly 50 percent down to 28 percent. Silicon Valley started to take off. New high-tech ventures began to get funding. Despite the sizeable rate cut, revenue from the capital gains levy went up.

Ronald Reagan took office with a keen awareness of America's tax burden and a desire to sharply ease it. To him, high income taxes were personal. At one point during his movie career, Reagan was told he shouldn't make more than two films a year. If he made more than two, he would jump into such a high tax bracket that he'd be left with little or no after-tax money on his earnings from the new movie. He thought it was absurd that we had a tax code that punished people who wanted to work more, to produce more.

Reagan signed two bold tax cuts into law: One in 1981, the next in 1986. The first lowered the top rate down to 50 percent and reduced other rates by about 25 percent. The second bill abolished numerous tax shelters and cut the number of tax brackets to two—28 percent and 15 percent.

These dramatic cuts pulled the U.S. out of the deep rut Reagan had inherited from the 1970s by increasing individual incentives to work more productively and to take more risks. Receipts from income taxes swelled. The American economy expanded by more than one-third during the Reagan years. In dollar terms, our growth exceeded the entire size of West Germany's economy, the world's third largest.[3] In 1980, the top 1 percent of income earners in America paid 18 percent of the federal government's tax receipts. By the time Reagan left office, that 1 percent was kicking in over 27 percent of those receipts. (Today, it's over 30 percent.)

The Reagan cuts illustrated a paradox most politicians can't fathom: Lower the tax rates and you get more tax money from the rich.

Why? With more reasonable tax rates, fewer top earners opted to expend time and effort on tax avoidance strategies aimed at achieving deductions. And so they took their pay the old fashioned way—as taxable income. People took more risks—which meant more investment, more innovation—and thus a larger tax base.

Reagan was able to get his tax bill passed in 1986 at the height of simplify-the-tax-code sentiment. Unfortunately, in the years to come, Washington politicians slid back into their bad habits—cluttering the code with new brackets, exemptions, deductions, phase-ins, phase-outs, and special breaks for special interests. Since Reagan's day, the code has been amended 14,000 times. Millions of new words were added, and the monster ballooned by nearly 60 percent.

This ever-increasing complexity has undermined our long-standing tradition of paying the taxes we owe. Even the most law-abiding individuals (as that infamous *Money* magazine survey made clear) couldn't be sure they were in compliance. Complexity has led to flagrant abuses of authority by the IRS, which finally prompted congressional hearings in 1997 and 1998 that led to a series of reforms. But make no mistake— as long as the code remains the monster it is today, voluntary compliance of paying taxes will be eroded and tax collecting abuses will emerge.

Sadly, too, the lessons of the Reagan years on the positive power of properly structured tax reductions were temporarily forgotten. His successor, George H.W. Bush, agreed to the Democrats' tax increase in 1990. The U.S. economy, already reeling from reduced defense spending and from the Savings-and-Loan banking collapse, promptly went into recession.

Recovery was initially slow. Not until the last six months of the Bush presidency did the economy exhibit any real signs of life. By then it was too late: Bush was defeated in 1992 by Bill Clinton on economic issues.

President Clinton raised taxes again in 1993. The nascent recovery was weakened. Taxpayers boosted their borrowings to help make up the income they lost to higher taxes. During Clinton's first year, the economy grew at a lower rate than it had under the last year of President Bush. This was a critical reason that Republicans won control of both houses of Congress in 1994, the first time the GOP had pulled off such as feat since 1952.

Thankfully, numerous other factors intervened in the 1990s to help revive the economy. They included the near-elimination of inflation; the

29 percent slash in the capital gains levy in 1997; the virtual elimination of capital gains taxes for most homes, triggering a housing boom that continues to this day; the moratorium on Internet taxation; welfare reform (signed by President Clinton under pressure from public opinion); and the North American Free Trade Agreement (NAFTA), which helped spur more trade with Mexico and Canada. The new GOP-controlled Congress, meanwhile, also helped control spending by the federal government.

But not all these initiatives were entirely successful. The 1997 tax bill Republicans forced on a reluctant President Clinton reduced the capital gains exaction from 28 percent to 20 percent. But it introduced new credits and other convoluted permutations that made the code still more complicated.

Clinton's successor, George W. Bush, is a genuine tax-cutter. However his first bill, passed in 2001, was relatively weak. Personal income-tax rate reductions, none too big in the first place, were phased in over a number of years. As a result, the legislation had little impact and produced disappointing results.

Bush's tax cut of 2003, however, was a dramatic improvement. The capital gains levy was cut from 20 percent to 15 percent, which meant that people would take more risks. The personal dividend tax was cut from 38 percent to 15 percent, meaning more capital creation. And the personal tax rate cuts of 2001 were made effective immediately— instead of being dribbled in over several years.

As a result of those measures, the economy improved as businesses responded to incentives to invest more. People had more money to pay their bills for the first time since the early 1990s. The percentage of their incomes applied to financing their debts began to fall.

Nonetheless, the beast is hardly in retreat. Full-time employment at the IRS is already 97,440 in fiscal year 2005! The tax code's complexity has grown; existing credits, like the one for children, have expanded and new credits have been created. They include limited deductions for college expenses, as well as credits for the purchase of electric vehicles and for the production of certain kinds of electricity.

The president's tax reductions, however, reflect his fundamental belief in tax simplification along the lines of a flat tax. The president tried to abolish the dividend tax for individuals, just as the flat tax would do. He also tried to get rid of the death tax, and he pushed for faster expensing of business capital expenditures. The president has also advocated tax reduction through the Lifetime Savings Accounts and Retirement Savings Accounts (LSAs and RSAs), two innovative super-savings vehicles. The RSA would allow individuals to put $5,000 each year in an account for retirement that would grow tax-free; withdrawals from the account—which could begin after age 58—would also be free from taxation. The other vehicle, the LSA, would permit individuals to put $5,000 annually into an account that would grow tax-free. But you could take the money out at anytime for any kind of expense.

Clearly President Bush is fully committed to a major overhaul of the tax code. Let's hope there will be no more half steps, that he will advocate an exciting, flat tax approach. If he drops the ball on genuine tax simplification and reduction, the Republicans may well pay the price in 2008. Entrepreneurial Democrats may finally ask themselves, "Why do we keep letting Republicans beat our brains out on taxes? Why not turn the tables on the GOP by stealing this issue right out from under them?" How? By advocating a flat tax. Unlikely? Politics has seen stranger things.

CHAPTER THREE

Complexity, Confusion, and Corruption: The Tax Code Is Ruining Our Quality of Life

Few people comprehend the true cost to the nation of the tax code. The tax dollars we pay are just the beginning. We also pay economically, socially, and psychologically.

The complexity and confusion of the current code corrupts our behavior and values and is ruining the quality of life for us as individuals and as a society.

For starters, there's the toll exacted based on the time and effort expended in preparing our returns: The countless hours spent compiling our records and filing out forms, with or without a tax preparer.

In a mere decade and a half, compliance costs in terms of your time spent have rocketed 67 percent. A typical taxpayer filing the regular

Form 1040, reporting income from work, dividends, and capital gains, will spend an average of 28 hours and 30 minutes each year completing a return. The same task 15 years ago took only 17 hours and 7 minutes.[1]

Billions of hours of lost productivity—the equivalent of 3.3 million fulltime jobs—are squandered on tax compliance. At last count, Americans spent a staggering 6.6 billion hours preparing their tax returns.

How does this mammoth effort translate into dollars? According to the Office of Management and Budget's estimate, compliance costs for the 2004 federal income tax will run to about $200 billion. This includes both actual monetary outlays to tax professionals, as well as the estimated labor costs you spend in readying your records for your tax preparer.

And that $200 billion does not include the aggravation involved in gathering the necessary records and information. The nights that we lay awake worrying: Did we take the right deductions? Or did we take too many? Do we have sufficient documentation? Did we provide the government with all the information they've requested on our sources of income? If we're in business, did we provide proper quarterly reports on our employee payments?

And the biggest worry of all: What if we're audited? There's the misery of having to dig out our records and endure endless examination and reexamination of present and past returns. Not to mention having to make hefty payments throughout the process to tax pros and tax lawyers and—if all else fails—exorbitant payments of back taxes and penalties, or worse.

In the first chapter, we saw examples of what can happen to taxpayers who endure this nightmare and end up in a dispute with the IRS. Once the agency comes after you, the process can be hard to stop, even when the IRS is wrong.

One such case was that of Delaware contractor Tom Savage, who was held accountable by the IRS for the unpaid taxes of a subcontractor that had no legal ties to him. Savage lost over $700,000 fighting the government, which placed a lien on his property. A Justice Department advisory that said the IRS had no case. But he nonetheless had to settle for $50,000.[2]

In the most extreme circumstances, tax tyranny can have tragic consequences: Edward Kugler endured a 10-year struggle with the IRS. He initially offered to pay part of $60,000 he owed and filed for bankruptcy on four separate occasions, but to no avail. His liability, with interest and penalties, eventually reached $155,000. Desperate, he took his own life by carbon monoxide poisoning.[3]

Confusion and more confusion. Little wonder that the prospect of running afoul of IRS regulations provokes such anxiety. You're never quite certain you're on solid footing, since the tax code is so abominably, appallingly *confusing*.

As we've seen, even the professionals are confounded by the code's jumble of regulations. Have you ever tried reading our tax code? Of course you haven't. Unless you're a tax pro, you probably shouldn't if you care to keep your sanity. If you're a better-than-average reader, you'd have to read for at least two months, eight hours a day, every day, to scale the code's nine million word mountain of verbiage.

Recall that our entire U.S. Constitution, which has served us for more than two hundred years, is a mere five thousand words, about two thousand times shorter.

Sadly brevity not one of the strengths of our tax code writers. Nor is clarity. Thus the code is littered with impenetrable passages like the following from the American Jobs Creation Act, the corporate tax bill passed by Congress in 2004. Read it—if you dare:

The conferees recognize that some taxpayers may own facilities at which the predominant activity is domestic production as defined in the conference agreement and other facilities at which they engage in the retail sale of the taxpayer's produced goods and also sell food and beverages. For example, assume that the taxpayer buys coffee beans and roasts those beans at a facility, the primary activity of which is the roasting and packaging of roasted coffee. The taxpayer sells the roasted coffee through a variety of unrelated third-party vendors and also sells roasted coffee at the taxpayer's own retail establishments. In addition, at the taxpayer's retail establishments, the taxpayer prepares brewed coffee and other foods. The conferees intend that to the extent that the gross receipts of the taxpayer's retail establishment represent receipts from the sale of its roasted coffee beans to customers, the receipts are qualified domestic production gross receipts, but to the extent that the gross receipts of the taxpayer's retail establishment represent receipts from the sale of brewed coffee or food prepared at the retail establishment, the receipts are not qualified domestic production gross receipts. However, the conferees intend that, in this case, the taxpayer may allocate part of the receipts from the sale of the brewed coffee as qualified domestic production gross receipts to the extent of the value of the roasted coffee beans used to brew the coffee. The conferees intend that the Secretary provide guidance drawing on the principles of section 482 by which such a taxpayer can allocate gross receipts between qualified and nonqualified gross receipts. The conferees observe that in this example, the taxpayer's sales of roasted coffee beans to unrelated third parties would provide a value for the beans used in brewing a cup of coffee for retail sale.

Would you believe this passage, all of three hundred words, is actually a footnote? It basically says that a hypothetical coffee maker can qualify for a new manufacturing tax break due to the fact that the business was involved in "roasting and packaging" coffee. This infamous loophole was inserted into the 2004 American Jobs Creation Act especially for Starbucks, which convinced legislators that it qualified as a "manufacturer" of coffee. The passage is the notorious "Starbucks provision," as outrageous for its favoritism as its assault on the English language.

The average individual seeking to navigate the code can feel like Alice after falling down the Rabbit Hole: Things simply get curiouser and curiouser.

A tangle of tax brackets. The individual income tax is a multi-headed hydra—with six different tax brackets and an avalanche of different personal exemptions and deductions. Your effective tax rate goes up as your income goes up. Once you figure out your rate, you then have to navigate a labyrinth of exemptions and deductions.

Federal Income Tax Rate Brackets

2004 Rate	Married Filing Jointly	Single	Head of Household
10%	0–$14,300	0–$7,150	0–$10,200
15%	$14,300–$58,100	$7,150–$29,050	$10,200–$38,900
25%	$58,100–$117,250	$29,050–$70,350	$38,900–$100,500
28%	$117,250–$178,650	$70,030–$146,750	$100,500–$162,700
33%	$178,650–$319,100	$146,750–$319,100	$162,700–$319,100
35%	Over $319,100	Over $319,100	Over $319,100

Try, if you can, to stay with us: You can elect to either take a standard deduction or itemize your deductions. The standard deduction depends on your status. If married, the standard deduction is $9,700, twice the single person's level of $4,850.

If you're the head of a household and a single parent, you get a $7,150 standard deduction. Adult and dependent exemptions come in at $3,100 per individual. Therefore, a family of four would multiply this number four times to get their personal-exemptions total. Then they'd add in either the standard deduction or the total sum of their itemized deductions. This makes up all the income that is untaxable.

A maze of deductions. Once you work your way through those basic exemptions, you're then faced with calculating deductions on mortgages; childcare; investment costs (including investment fees, custodial fees, trust administration fees, as well as other expenses incurred in managing investments to produce income); education expenses; work-related expenses; interest expenses; losses from theft or casualty; state or local taxes paid; medical expenses; moving expenses; contributions to charities; gambling losses (yes, it's true—gambling losses can be deducted up to the amount of gambling winnings, which themselves

Tax Provisions Enacted in the Economic Growth and Tax Relief Reconciliation 2002, and the Jobs and Growth Tax Relief Reconciliation Act of 2003, by

Description	Pre-EGTRRA	2001	2002	2003	2004
Tax Rates and Brackets					
10 Percent Tax Bracket	n.a.	Single filers may have income of up to $6,000; joint filers, $12,000; and heads of household, $10,000		Single filers, up of household	
15 Percent Tax Bracket	Indexed				
Higher Tax Brackets (Percent)	39.6 36 31 28	39.1 35.5 30.5 27.5	38.6 35 30 27	35 (38.6) 33 (35) 28 (30) 25 (27)	35 (37.6) 33 (34) 28 (29) 25 (26)
Rate on Capital Gains	10 percent for taxpayers in the 15 percent bracket or below; 20 percent for other taxpayers			After May 6, 2003, 5 percent and 0 in 2008; 15 percent	
Rate on Dividends	Ordinary rates			5 percent for taxpayers in taxpayers (Ordinary rates)	
				Limitations on Itemized Deductions	
Change in Limitations	No change				
Child Credit and Dependent Care Credit					
Child Credit	$500, with limited refundability	$600 Refundable up to 10 percent of earned income above $10,000; threshold indexed after 2001		$1,000	
Dependent Care Credit	Maximum expenditure eligible for credit = $2,400 for one child and $4,800 for two or more; maximum credit = 20 percent to 30 percent of expenditures		Maximum of $3,000 of eligible expenses for Maximum credit of 35 percent, phasing down		
Relief from Marriage Penalties					
Standard Deduction for Joint Filers	Standard deduction for joint filers = 167 percent of that for single filers				
15 Percent Bracket for Joint Filers	Upper threshold of bracket for those who are married filing jointly = 167 percent of the top of the bracket for single filers				
Earned Income Credit for Joint Filers	Level of income at which the earned income credit starts to phase out is indexed; end of phaseout depends on number of children	Starting point and ending point of phaseout are increased by $1,000			
Relief from Alternative Minimum Tax					
Exemption for the Alternative Minimum Tax	$33,750 for single filers; $45,000 for joint filers	$35,750 for single filers; $49,000 for joint filers		$40,250 for single filers; $58,000 for joint filers ($35,750; $49,000)	
Partial Expensing of Investment in Qualified Property					
Depreciation Deduction of Basis of Qualified Property	No additional depreciation	30 percent of basis deductible in first year (After Sept. 10, 2001)		50 percent of basis deductible in first year	

Notes: Parenthetical Values are those set by EGTRRA   * = Provision returns to pre-EGTRRA levels

Act of 2001, the Job Creation and Worker Assistance Act of Year, Pre-2001 through 2011

2005	2006	2007	2008	2009	2010	2011
to $7,000; joint filers, $14,000; and heads $10,000; indexed in 2004 ($6,000;$12,000;$10,000)				Upper and lower thresholds indexed		Sunset*
		35 33 28 25				Sunset*
for taxpayers in the 15 percent bracket or below-- for other taxpayers (10 percent; 20 percent)						Sunset*
the 15 percent bracket or below--and 0 in 2008; 15 percent for other						Sunset*
and Personal Exemptions for High-Income Filers						
	Limits reduced by one-third		Limits reduced by two-thirds		No limits	Sunset*
Refundable up to 15 percent of earned income above $10,000; threshold indexed after 2001						Sunset*
one child; $6,000 for two or more children to 20 percent beginning at $15,000 in adjusted gross income						Sunset*
200 percent of that for single filers						Sunset*
200 percent of that for single filers						Sunset*
Starting point and ending point of phaseouts are increased by $2,000			Starting point and ending point are increased by $3,000	Starting point and ending point are increased by $3,000; indexed from 2008		Sunset*
						Sunset*
						Sunset*

Sources: Congressional Budget Office. "Effective Federal Tax Rates Under Current Law, 2001 to 2014," August 2004. Joint Committee on Taxation. Estimated Revenue Effects of the Conference Agreement For H.R. 1308, The "Working Families Tax Relief Act of 2004" September 23, 2004.

must be reported to the IRS); tax preparation fees—and the list goes on and on.

Yes, it's a veritable cornucopia of tax breaks. But, as we all know, we can't always take them. Complicated rules allow the government to phase out many deductions and even personal exemptions in certain income categories. For example, married higher-income taxpayers who file jointly must reduce their use of personal exemptions by 2 percent for each $2,500 ($1,250 for married filing separately) of adjusted gross income over $214,050. The exemption is completely phased out by $336,550. These income thresholds are different for singles, heads of households, or married people who file separate returns.

Hold on, things get more complicated: Beginning in 2006, the reduction of personal exemptions will be gradually phased out. (They will be reinstated after 2010 if the Bush tax cuts are not made permanent.) Various itemized deductions are also subject to phase outs. Deductions for state and local taxes are phased out at $139,500 for married couples filing jointly.

And then here's the kicker: If your income is high enough, you lose up to 80 percent of these itemized deductions. But there is good news: medical expenses, casualty and theft losses, investment interest expenses, and, yes, gambling losses are not subject to the itemized-deduction phase out.

Just take a gander at the previous table. Mind-boggling, isn't it? And don't forget, Congress changes many of these numbers each year.

What most people don't realize is that the phase out of such deductions is an effective increase in the highest tax rate. You, the taxpayer, still pays the same 35 percent. But that's now 35 percent of a larger amount of taxable income.

Some other examples:

- The child tax credit is phased out at $50 per $1,000 of additional income at $110,000 for a couple.

- The Alternative Minimum Tax (AMT) exemption of $58,000 for married couples is phased out at $150,000.
- Lifetime learning/HOPE credit is phased out at $85,000 for a couple.
- Personal exemptions are phased out for single people between $142,700—$265,000; joint/married—$214,000—$336,500; separate returns but married—$107,025—$168,275; head of household—$178,350—$300,850.
- Traditional IRA deductions are phased out at $65,000 of income per couple, $45,000 for a single person.

On and on it goes.

The Medicare Tax is also biting hard now. There is no income cap on this 2.9 percent tax. You pay that 2.9 percent on all of your non-investment income. (The Social Security wages cap is at $90,000.)

Wait a minute, do you work here? Another example tax code complexity is one that regularly befuddles business owners: IRS criteria for determining who is an employee of their business. These distinctions, of course, are crucial to determining whether an employer is responsible for a worker's payroll taxes. The IRS classifies people "performing services" for a business into several different categories: independent contractors, common-law employees, statuary employees, and statuary nonemployees.

In the IRS guide for employers, there are three main headings for qualifying workers. They are "behavioral control, financial control, and type of relationship."

Figuring out which category your employee comes under involves evaluating numerous factors for each one. Only after you get through all this can you then determine whether or not the worker is an "employee" or an "independent contractor." But the real chore hasn't even begun. The next task is figuring out how much taxes must be paid or held back as withholding.

If you still don't feel confident about whether you are paying an "employee" or an "independent contractor," you can fill out a Form

SS-8—which consists of three pages and over fifty questions. The IRS will then provide your answer. That is, if you can trust them.

Is anyone at all surprised by a recent Associated Press poll that found that 7 in 10 people believe their federal taxes are too complicated? And 49 percent said they'd prefer a trip to the dentist to preparing their tax returns.

With all the lawsuits today over stress in the work place, it's remarkable there are no lawsuits over the emotional duress caused by having to cope with this chaos.

CODE CONFUSION HURTS LOW-INCOME PEOPLE

The tax code does more than massively squander time and emotional energy. It hurts the very people it has been designed to help.

Tax code confusion is not only costly for low income people who must pay the costs of a tax preparer. It prevents them from identifying—and getting—much needed tax breaks.

A study by the University of California found that, in California, only 36 percent of eligible Latinos actually receive the federal Earned-Income Tax Credit (EITC).[4] The EITC is supposed to create incentives to stay in the workplace and off welfare, while helping people on welfare to make a successful transition to the workplace. The EITC can amount to more than $4,000 of extra cash to those eligible, even when no taxes are owed to the government. Why haven't more eligible individuals gone for this free money? Because they've never heard about it.

Low-income families—not to mention most everyone else—are made up of hardworking people who don't have the time or energy to keep up with complicated, constantly changing tax issues. They don't have the money to invest in consulting tax lawyers to discover how the tax code may benefit them.

The EITC requires the taxpayers to file an additional schedule. To make sure that the filer understands how the EITC works, IRS Publication 596 is supposed to tell people how to claim the EITC and go about getting it. Problem is: The document is fifty pages long, containing 25,000 words of tax-filing "help."

When filing for the EITC, taxpayers have to sift through bewildering instructions to determine whether they're eligible. Is their child a "qualifying child" who will allow them to get the tax break—and if so, according to which tax credit under this confusing law?

How is a struggling single mother living from paycheck to paycheck supposed to cope with that? According to the IRS, 62 percent of EITC taxpayers use preparers, many of whom provide their services on a pro bono basis. But then why do only about a third of Latinos, a key group for whom the credit was intended, manage to get it?

The statistic illustrates our point: A tax credit intended to help the working poor should be designed to be accessible.

Then there are people who receive the EITC but should not. An estimated $6.5 billion to $10 billion in EITC payments each year may be improper. That's about one-fourth of the dollars spent on the program.[5]

David Cay Johnson writes about one taxpayer who earned $91,000 and still managed to "qualify" for the maximum amount of the EITC because he earned most of his income in dividends and was able to off-set these earnings by a paper loss.[6]

The reason for this fraud is that the complexity of the EITC encourages scams, such as bogus tax preparers who file returns in the names of often unwitting low-income taxpayers and pocket the money. Not long ago two San Diego sisters were sentenced to prison for claiming $8.7 million in false payments by filing fraudulent tax returns on behalf of their supposed clients.

The bottom line: tax credits designed to help low-income families and individuals get off and stay off welfare are so convoluted and obscure that both fraud and unclaimed benefits are commonplace.

Studies reveal an ironic reality: that lower-income families are hit hardest by the cost of tax compliance.

According to a study by the Tax Foundation, those with incomes of less than $20,000 a year pay a compliance cost equal to 4.5 percent of their taxable incomes, while those whose taxable income is in the $40,000–$75,000 range pay only 1.3 percent of their incomes for such services.[7] According to the report, savings from tax simplification would have the greatest benefit to those with incomes under $20,000.

Few people are aware of the extent to which our behavior, each and every day, is influenced by the tax code and our continuing effort to reduce what we owe Uncle Sam.

Think about it. How many activities do you find yourself engaging in purely "for tax purposes?" You hasten charitable contributions, postpone income, donate old clothing, prepay property taxes. You do things you wouldn't ordinarily do, from traveling on vacation to business meetings you wouldn't ordinarily attend (enabling you to take a tax deduction), to selling stock you wouldn't otherwise, or prematurely transferring major assets, such as your home, into the names of your children while you're relatively healthy and not quite ready to do so.

Financial publications including *Forbes* and others tell us each year how to reduce taxes by a variety of strategies—from estate planning to the best ways to deduct your alimony payments.

The tax code influences our activities as consumers. We're all familiar with how tax credits encourage certain types of behavior, such as home buying, while discouraging others, such as consuming high-tax items like tobacco.

If Larry Jones, who lives in Haverhill, Massachusetts, near the New Hampshire border, wants to buy a new hot tub for his back deck, he will shop around for the best price. Since New Hampshire has no state sales tax, chances are that if he finds a comparably priced hot tub in New Hampshire, he'll buy it there instead of in Massachusetts. Why fork over the hundreds of extra dollars in sales tax?

Larry's behavior is a classic example of taxes affecting decision-making. In much the same way, the federal income tax code alters the daily decisions of millions of Americans. The tax code's complex assortment of rates and deductions, favoring certain types of investment or behavior, produce a distorting effect on the economy with far-reaching ramifications.

Case in point: the effects of the 1981 Economic Recovery Act. Among other things, this legislation liberalized the rules for commercial real estate depreciation and capital gains taxes. Properties, for instance, could be depreciated in fifteen years instead of forty. Smart companies like General Electric were able to reduce their tax liabilities to zero.

The result? Real estate investing became the tax shelter of choice, creating artificial demand and an explosion in the building of commercial space. Dallas alone saw office space skyrocket by an astounding 246 percent.[8] By the end of the 1980s, office space in America had doubled and outstanding commercial property debt had tripled.[9]

Then came the 1986 Tax Reform Act, which erased the tax advantages of the 1981 reform, thus discouraging individuals and companies from investing in commercial properties. Capital suddenly evaporated, leaving the industry looking like a parched riverbed after a drought. Commercial real estate market values withered, particularly in Texas, where rents fell by half.

This collapse helped precipitate the nationwide Savings-and-Loan crisis, resulting in the failure of 747 S&Ls over the next six years. More than $519 billion in assets were lost due to the closings of 1,043

Major Tax Law Provisions Affecting Returns on Commercial Real Estate Investment

	Pre-Economic Recovery Tax Act of 1981	Post-Economic Recovery Tax Act of 1981	Post-Tax Reform Act of 1986
Allowable depreciation life, commercial real estate	40 Years	15 Years	31.5 Years
Allowable depreciation method	Straight-line	175% Decline balance	Straight-line
Passive losses deductible?	Yes	Yes	No
Max. ordinary income tax rate	70%	50%	38.5%
Capital gains tax rate	28%	20%	28%

Source: FDIC. *History of the Eighties – Lessons for the Future*, 1997, pg. 163.

institutions, mainly through speculative investment schemes prompted by tax incentives.[10]

That's not to say that taxes can't be a positive force. Once again the real estate industry provides an example: the residential housing boom that occurred after the virtual elimination of capital gains on residences in 1997.

According to the National Association of Realtors' median sales prices of existing homes, the price of a home increased about 27 percent in the six years before the capital gains tax exclusion was expanded to include virtually all homeowners. In the six years following, housing prices rose nearly 47 percent, creating a thriving market that is still with us today.

Politicians are well aware of these effects on our behavior. They're all too quick to use the code to run our lives—and expand their influence.

Washington's tax writers have in the past twenty years mitigated a lot of the good done by Ronald Reagan's tax simplification. They've added countless amendments, credits, and special breaks—causing the Internal Revenue code and its attendant regulations to mushroom by more than 57 percent.[11]

Unable to resist the opportunity to engineer social policy, politicians in the intervening years have passed law upon law. During the Clinton presidency, there was the expansion of the earned-income credit, new educational tax credits, new child tax credits, and more.

Both the Bush and Clinton administrations have egregiously cluttered the tax code. Clinton favored tax breaks that encouraged more government social engineering; President Bush tends to support provisions that encourage economic growth and business investment. But he has nonetheless added his share to the confusion: The tax code has grown each year he has held office. Some of the novel deductions on his watch include credits for purchasing new hybrid cars—a $2,000 credit for anyone who bought one of these clean-fuel modes of transportation. The idea that people might simply buy such vehicles for their obvious benefits was beyond the understanding of our nanny-minded tax writers. About the only thing missing from the code today is a tax credit for not eating Twinkies.

Of course, President Bush helped the economy enormously with his 2003 tax cut. This new law, among other things, reduced the capital gains levy and, through a host of other measures, is making the U.S. once again the world's fastest-growing economy among large and developed nations. But the increasing tax code complexity during his administration has kept the economy from doing even better.

All the layers upon layers of regulations and tax breaks imposed by both administrations no doubt have provided relief to some quarters— like the housing boom that occurred after the 1997 near-elimination of residential capital gains. However, despite such short-term benefits, what our present tax code produces is mostly distortion—distortion of our individual behavior and of the market—that, in the long term, usually produces negative consequences.

WORK AND PRODUCTIVITY ARE DISCOURAGED

Upon reaching the highest tax bracket, wage earners have less incentive to be productive in the workplace. As we will see later in this chapter, the marginal tax rate takes increasingly larger chunks of each additional dollar earned. Consequently, the will to work decreases.

Ronald Reagan, as we've mentioned, learned this in his acting days. (See chapter two.) He limited his work schedule upon realizing he would suffer severe tax penalties for making more than two movies a year.

If taxpayers were not financially penalized for their increased income, they would be much more likely to allocate their time to working and saving, and boosting productivity. They would be less likely to engage in leisure activities and consumption.

Nobel Prize-winning economist Edward Prescott has shown the effect that high taxes have on a country's workers.[12] Prescott examined the question: Why do Americans work so much more than Europeans?

His findings reveal that Americans work 50 percent more than their counterparts in France, Germany, and Italy. Very high tax rates in those countries persuade people to work less. These findings also hold true for non-Western cultures like Japan.

Prescott demonstrated that, historically, *when the French and others were taxed similarly to Americans, they worked the same amount of time*. Europeans only began to work less as their tax rates increased, creating today's huge disparity between American and European productivity.

TRUST IN GOVERNMENT IS CORRODED

The inequities and distortions produced by the tax code undermine the social contract, our collective faith in society's values and institutions. An IRS report to Congress voiced concern that such loss of trust could one day impede the agency's ability to function: "If taxpayers ever lose confidence that their friends, neighbors and business competitors are paying their fair share of taxes, then they could become less willing to pay themselves."[13]

For many people, this loss of confidence is already a reality, a result of the wild disparities produced by today's tax code.

What is fair, for instance, about allowing a person to pay lower taxes than his neighbor because he bought a gas/electric hybrid car? Until recently, the marriage penalty was another glaring example of how our tax system failed the fairness test. It forced married couples to pay more in taxes than unmarried couples who lived together and made the same amount of money.

President Bush reduced the marriage penalty by increasing the standard deduction for married couples and temporarily expanding the size of their tax brackets. The *Boston Globe* reported on the effects of the change, "… two singles, each earning $35,000 in 2004 might erase a penalty of $948 that they would have faced under the old law after getting married. A higher-income couple in which each spouse earns $70,000 would still pay a penalty for marriage but only $206 instead of $1,600."[14]

That's progress, but not enough when compared to the fairness of the flat tax, with its across the board tax rate of 17 percent, after generous exemptions for adults and children.

But the problem is not just inequities. We have grown so accepting of our servitude to the tax beast that we rarely ever stop and ask: Just how fair are these taxes in the first place?

For example, how fair is it to tax the Social Security benefits that you've already spent your lifetime paying for with tax dollars? That's right, you're paying tax on a tax! Say a worker earns $50,000—his share of his social security tax is $3,100. (His employer pays another $3,100.) Yet that worker still pays income taxes on that $3,100 even though he never got that money.

Now consider what happens when you start to draw your Social Security benefits: If your Adjusted Gross Income* exceeds $32,000 for a couple and $25,000 for an individual, then half of your Social Security benefits are subject to the federal income tax. If your Adjusted Gross Income exceeds $44,000 ($32,000 for an individual) then an astounding 85 percent of your Social Security benefits are subject to federal income tax.

That's Washington for you. Earn $44,000 a year and you're "rich." But not for long, if they have anything to say about it.

In addition to having to endure the singular indignity of paying a tax on a tax under our beastly federal code, you're also punished for financially responsible behavior, i.e. saving for retirement.

The federal income tax code taxes capital gains, dividends, interest payments, and all non-Roth IRA withdrawals from retirement accounts. Dividends and capital gains are taxed at 5 percent for taxpayers in the 10 percent to 15 percent tax brackets and at 15 percent for all other taxpayers.

Don't think it's all over after retirement. As we're all acutely aware, Uncle Sam gets you coming and going, thanks to the death tax. Under the current tax code, estates over $1.5 million are subject to a top tax rate of 47 percent.

There are multiple brackets here, too. They start at 18 percent and rise rapidly to 32 percent and then rise more gradually to the top rate. The death tax is being phased out and will cease to exist in the year 2010.

---

*Income adjusted down by IRS-specified deductions, but not including standard and itemized deductions. AGI is the number you write at the bottom of page 1 of the 1040 form that is copied to the top of page 2.

But it will rise again in 2011 at 50 percent for all estates over $1 million. A one-year reprieve is hardly a step toward sustained tax reform.

THE ALTERNATIVE MINIMUM TAX: YOU PAY THE MAXIMUM

If all of this wasn't unfair enough, many taxpayers must face the added insult of the Alternative Minimum Tax (AMT). Its original intent was to make sure wealthy individuals taking large deductions did not escape paying income taxes. Today the AMT affects increasingly large numbers of middle-income taxpayers. Thanks to its disorientating rules and special provisions, you end up losing your personal exemptions, standard deductions and state and local tax deductions, in addition to an assortment of other tax deductions.

When it was first enacted in 1970, the AMT ensnared 19,000 households. Today, more than *3 million Americans* pay the AMT.[15] Astonishingly, more than 30 million middleclass families could be liable for the AMT by 2010.

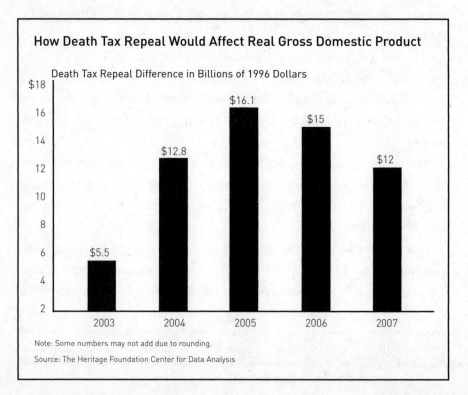

How Death Tax Repeal Would Affect Real Gross Domestic Product

Death Tax Repeal Difference in Billions of 1996 Dollars

Note: Some numbers may not add due to rounding.

Source: The Heritage Foundation Center for Data Analysis

This year (2005) it kicks in for those who have adjusted gross incomes that are more than $58,000 (married filing jointly). Around 27 percent of households making between $75,000—$100,000 will pay the AMT in 2005.[16]

But it only gets worse. AMT rates are levied at 26 percent to 28 percent. Taxpayers must figure out their tax liability twice to see whether they have to pay the AMT—or their regular income tax. By doubling the work that AMT payers must do to file their tax returns, the tax code is punishing higher-income earners with greater complexity. They have to devote more time and dollars to do their more complicated returns.

According to the Treasury Department's Taxpayers Advocate, 80 percent of AMT taxpayers pay someone to calculate and prepare their taxes, while on average, about 62 percent of all taxpayers use a paid preparer.[17]

Little wonder that the IRS itself feared that the tax system would collapse under the weight of this unfairness. Making matters worse, even the people who run the system can't make sense of it—and you're responsible for their mistakes.

Treasury Department audits of the IRS's toll-free tax law telephone-assistance program found that the answers provided by the IRS's specialists were wrong 27 percent of the time.[18] What makes this worse is that even if the IRS gives you the wrong answer, you have no recourse but to pay for their error, along with any penalties and interest accrued. In short, you are still required to pay what IRS claims you owe—a policy that not only undermines confidence but fuels resentment.

If you decide to turn to a private concern such as H&R Block, or maybe Turbo Tax's website, to find the answer, you won't necessarily be better off. According to a *Wall Street Journal* report, these services actually fare worse on tax questions than the IRS's website.[19]

Most Americans are patriotic and would comply fully—though not necessarily happily—with their federal income tax obligations if only the rules were clear. Instead they're faced with a muddle of directives, with no one in authority able to deal with them.

NO ONE IS EXEMPT FROM TAX CODE UNFAIRNESS:
A TALE OF TWO PRESIDENTS

Even former presidents have to endure the unfairness of the code. Take the vastly differing fortunes of former Presidents Eisenhower and Truman after they wrote their memoirs.

Prior to his presidency, Dwight Eisenhower commanded American and Allied Forces in Europe during World War II and led us to victory over Nazi Germany. Before he became our thirty-fourth president, Ike wrote his military memoirs, *Crusade in Europe*, reaping a huge windfall because of special tax treatment.

President Truman, as a favor to the much admired general, had made sure that the IRS ruled to treat royalties from the book as capital gains, not as normal earned income. As a result, Eisenhower raked in $476,000, which was $300,000 more than he would have received had the payment been considered normal income.

But when Harry Truman wrote *his* memoirs, he made a paltry $37,000. Why? Because a change in the 1950 Revenue Act, "The Eisenhower Amendment," intended to eliminate the general's special tax break. Truman paid a steep price for his generosity to Ike: Instead of a low capital gains rate, he was hit by confiscatory rates as high as 91 percent.[20]

The story shows the extreme inequities produced by the tax code that can triple one man's earnings while wreaking havoc on another's. Eisenhower's book royalties shouldn't have been sheltered from taxation, but neither should Truman's have been stifled by morbidly high rates.

With the flat tax we would worry less about Eisenhower-like tax shelters because taxpayers would not need to run for cover each tax season.

LOOPHOLES AND TAX SHELTERS PRODUCE USELESS
ECONOMIC ACTIVITY THAT COSTS YOU MONEY

Twenty years ago, President Reagan signed the Tax Reform Act of 1986, which swept away numerous tax loopholes and instituted a two-bracket system. The tax shelter industry suffered a heavy loss. But like an obnoxious relative who always keeps coming back to visit, tax complexity returned with a vengeance.

By the 1990s, the code had once more become a rule-encrusted thicket, giving rise to a proliferation of what are referred to as "abusive" tax shelters. These shelters are different than the common, straightforward strategies designed to take advantage of deductions. They're the quintessential products and vehicles of tax code distortion: Convoluted entities and transactions created for the sole purpose of avoiding taxes. Most were designed for corporations. Financial losses that existed only on paper would be manufactured to offset tax liabilities. At least real estate tax shelters gave us actual buildings.

The Government Accountability Office of the U.S. government released a report noting that, since 1993, the government has lost $85 billion in tax payments because of abusive tax shelters—money that could have been returned to you, the people.[21]

According to the Government Accountability Office, some 6,400 individuals and corporations "bought abusive tax shelters and other abusive tax planning products" in recent years.

Our code is so convoluted that government efforts to collect back taxes from these tax-avoidance schemes have often faltered in the courts, with judges repeatedly ruling against the IRS on these issues. As abusive as these shelters may be, thanks to our 9-million-word tax monster, they're apparently legal.

These tax shelters not only lead to pressure to tax the rest of us at higher rates, but also wasted the brainpower of some of America's best minds who created them. Peter Cobb, former deputy chief of staff of the Joint Committee on Taxation observed, "You can't underestimate how many of America's greatest minds right now are being devoted to what economists would all say is totally useless economic activity."[22] Our system is broken to the point that it has created a drain on our intellectual capital.

Not that the strategies aren't ingenious. A few years back, Black and Decker created a new company, Black and Decker Health Care

Management, ostensibly to manage employee health care, then used the company to create a paper loss. In 1998, the parent company transferred $560 million in potential employee health care claims along with $561 million in cash to the new subsidiary. In return, the company gave Black and Decker $561 million in stock, which in turn was "sold" for $1 million to a former company executive.

The $560 million loss from the sale of the subsidiary's stock was eventually used to offset a $670 million gain from the sale of other parts of the company. All told, the entire business netted Black and Decker $180 million in tax savings.

The IRS attempted to challenge Black and Decker, but eventually lost, based on the fact that, according to the court, the transaction involved economic substance since the healthcare management subsidiary indeed provided some form of service. Yet Black and Decker admitted that it executed the transaction simply for tax avoidance purposes.

A *Baltimore Sun* journalist wrote, "Black and Decker's money basically made a round trip, doing a drive-by mugging of the IRS on the way."[23]

Another equally outrageous example was mentioned in chapter one: the corporate tax act signed in October 2004, informally known as the "No Lobbyist Left Behind Act." What was initially to have been a simple adjustment to a foreign tax subsidy turned into $140 billion in tax giveaways. There are tax breaks for professional golfers, racetrack owners, cruise lines, and "manufacturers" like Starbucks (getting that infamous tax break for the coffee grinding component of its business).

Of course, among the biggest tax abuse stories of the last ten years is the Enron scandal. According to *New York Times* reporter David Cay Johnson, the energy company "created 881 subsidiaries abroad, almost all of them tax havens, including 692 in the Cayman Islands, 199 in the Turks and Caicos, 43 in Mauritius, 8 in Bermuda and 19 others... Enron used tax shelters that allowed it to report $2 billion in profits almost immediately, even as the company was saving $2 billion of federal income tax over a period of years."[24]

The flat tax would eliminate the possibility of setting up complicated tax-avoidance schemes. The code would be too transparent, too simple to hide tax liabilities.

Former House of Representatives Majority Leader Dick Armey had it right: "The flat tax would have a chilling effect on the lobbying industry and would transform the entire political culture in Washington."

THE ULTIMATE TAX CODE DISTORTION: OUR HEALTH CARE SYSTEM

Few people realize that today's widely criticized health care system is in fact the ultimate product of tax code distortion.

A little history: Companies began paying for workers' health insurance during World War II as a way of paying their skilled workers more than was allowed at the time under existing wage and price controls.

While the practice was no longer necessary after the war, it captured the imagination of tax policy makers and social engineers: Companies should be allowed to deduct health care premiums, they asserted, to encourage more corporations to pay for their employees' health care.

The intent was to free up corporate dollars to underwrite more healthcare for more people. But the social engineers, well meaning as they were, didn't foresee the unintended consequences of this tax break. It created a disconnect between health care providers and consumers. No longer were most health care consumers making buying decisions based on the cost and value of services. Instead, third parties—corporate or government employers and insurance companies—were paying.

Result: Consumers whose healthcare was paid for by third parties no longer felt the need for restraint. Demand for healthcare soared. Costs ballooned out of control.

Even worse, the kinds of cost-reducing innovations we see in other industries, particularly in high tech, were—and still are—largely absent in health care.

If third party payments had not been fueled by tax breaks, we may never have found ourselves with the system we have today. Among the solutions proposed are health savings accounts—HSAs—that would encourage the return of market forces to healthcare by allowing employees to pay through tax free savings accounts. [See Appendix C.]

In the occasional instances where free market forces have been allowed to work, health care costs in fact decrease. A prime example is that of laser eye surgery, which is not usually covered by insurance. Consumers, whose buying choices are in part based on cost, have kept prices down. Such an operation today costs about a third of what it did ten years ago.

In much the same way, a flat tax, which would eliminate distortion-producing healthcare deductions, would restore the connection between the healthcare provider and the consumer. It would allow us to get control of runaway health care costs. With consumers in charge, healthcare would become more affordable—and more available.

The flat tax is the only way to bring back sanity and put an end to the clutter, confusion, and distortions of the current system. Clamoring for smarter tax software, better trained IRS staff and targeted tax cuts will never solve our tax problems. Neither will complaining about accountants' high fees when there are discrepancies in your tax return. Ultimately, no proposed solution will address these concerns unless the code is dramatically simplified. Most of the so-called answers only further mess up the code. However well-intended they may be, tax credits such as limited deductions of college expenses or for dependent care only add to the distortion. And their benefits aren't felt equally by all working Americans.

As long as politicians keep tinkering with taxes to suit their political ends, we'll have ever more chaos to cope with at tax-filing time.

By reducing the complexity and costs of complying with the tax laws, a flat tax would, in effect, give Americans a huge tax cut. Even if the flat tax only reduced compliance costs by half, that would amount to a reduction of $100 billion. That $100 billion is half of what the "massive" Bush tax cuts supposedly will cost for the year 2005.[25]

CHAPTER FOUR

How the Forbes Flat Tax Will Free America

So how do we end the confusion, clutter, and corruption—the angst and misery of having to prepare and pay our federal income taxes? If you read the previous chapters, you have no doubt reached the conclusion: Small fixes and tinkering won't work. The current system is hopeless.

We must kill the tax monster, drive a stake through its heart to ensure it never rises again. We must replace it with a fair and simple flat tax system.

Come tax time, your return would be completed by filling out a single sheet of paper or postcard. Only then will we see real, lasting reform.

The Forbes flat tax will accomplish this. It will throw out today's federal income tax code. It will eliminate the confusion, anxiety, and discomfort that are part of the process of filing and paying our taxes. It will do away with the corruption and economic distortion produced by the current system.

The flat tax will free America. It will liberate us, as individuals and as a society, from the tyranny of the federal tax code.

The Forbes Flat Tax is a single-rate federal income tax and corporate tax of 17 percent. Income is taxed as close to the source as possible. No more double or triple taxation. Income is taxed once and only once. No more effort-sapping, discouragingly high tax rates. Just one, simple rate.

All the information you need to file will fit on a simple card or sheet of paper. With the flat tax, there's no need to muddle over twenty-page tax tables. No more filling out page upon page of confusing returns.

The flat tax would replace today's federal income tax code, the biggest portion of the tax burden for half the population and the most abusive part of our tax system. (It does not supplant Medicare and Social Security taxes or, obviously, state and local taxes.) It is a first, major step towards a total overhaul of the entire American tax system.

Among key features of the flat tax:

Generous and refundable exemptions for adults and children. The flat tax eradicates the clutter of varying rates and deductions. It does retain a limited number of basic exemptions for children and adults that have been part of our tax system for decades. However the flat tax version of these deductions is more generous. Here's how they'll work:

- *Adults would be able to take a $13,200 standard exemption.* Single people who make less than that would come right off the tax rolls.
- *Married couples would receive a $26,400 deduction ($13,200 x 2).* No penalty at all for being married. Heads of households such as single mothers would have a 30 percent higher exemption of $17,160 to compensate for the additional burden of raising a child alone.
- *Families would receive generous exemptions for dependents:* a $4,000 exemption for each child or dependent, and a refundable tax credit of

$1,000 per child age 16 or younger. Parents of eligible children will receive the $1,000 tax credit for each child, as under the current system.

In addition, another feature of the current code—one that's a bit complicated—would remain: If the child tax credit exceeds federal taxes owed, the family can receive a refund. For example, if a family makes $15,000 but paid zero dollars of tax they can still receive $600 of the child credit (15 percent of the $4,000 of income over $11,000), even though they paid absolutely no federal income tax.

We retain this complex relic of today's code—tacked on the monster in 2001—to ensure that no one would pay more under the flat tax than he or she does under the current code.

All you'd have to do to get the refund is fill out that one-page tax form. The refund would work just like the current child tax credit.

A family of four would pay no federal income tax on its first $46,165 of income. In fact, they might receive a small rebate from the government. For instance, if that family of four had a tough year during and annual income came in at $40,000, it would receive a tax "refund" of $1,048 from the IRS.

That $46,165 for the family of four is more than twice the current federal poverty level. A family of six—mom, dad, and four kids—would owe no income tax until its earnings exceeded $65,930

Once again, these deductions are far more generous than those available under our current system. Today, taxpayers start with just a $3,100 exemption. Single persons who do not itemize can only take an additional $4,850 deduction for a total of $7,950. A single head of household can take an extra $7,150 or $10,250 total ($3,100 plus $7,150). Contrast this with the flat tax's standard exemption for each adult of $13,200.

Thanks to the elimination of the marriage penalty during President Bush's first term, a married couple now takes a standard deduction of $9,700, in addition to two $3,100 exemptions—for a $15,900 total. Which would you rather have: a $15,900 exemption or a $26,400 exemption under the flat tax?

Flat Tax Rate Table

	Single Mother	Middle-Class Family*	Professional Couple*
Income	$25,000	$50,000	$150,000
Taxable income	$3,350	$14,800	$123,600
	($25,000 – $21,650)	($50,000 – $35,200)	($150,000 – $27,000)
Tax paid	$-414 (17% x $3350, minus child credit)	$550 (17% x $14,800, minus child credits)	$20,910 (17% x $123,000)
Effective tax rate	-1.7%	1.1%	13.9%

*Assumes a married couple filing jointly in 2006.

Flat-tax deductions for a family of four are almost $11,000 more generous than those the current code provides.

In addition to the child tax credit, my flat tax allows for the retention of the Earned Income Tax Credit (EITC), a feature of today's tax code that is aimed at helping low-income families with children. The EITC is a back-door way of effectively refunding their Social Security and Medicare taxes. Any change in the EITC must be part of a package of Social Security reforms.

That's the basic plan—just a 17 percent tax rate after generous exemptions. Perhaps as you read this you are already feeling lighter, imagining the heavy weight of the Beast lifting off your back.

The idea is simple, but it has massive implications for us as taxpayers:

The flat tax is a tax cut. Anyway you slice it, your tax bill will be reduced under the plan. Think of what you're paying now. Then compare that to what you'd owe under the flat tax.

There's also the huge indirect tax cut that the flat tax will deliver by reducing the costs of complying with our tortuous tax laws. Even if the flat tax only reduced compliance costs by half, that would amount, as we've said, to a reduction of $100 billion. Remember that $100 billion is half of what the "massive" Bush tax cuts supposedly will cost for the year 2005.[1]

Under the flat tax, 65 million returns—or 42 percent of all returns—would owe no tax by the year 2010. That's right. We'll say it again: Millions of lower-income people will not have to pay any tax. This part of the flat tax is in line with the original intent of our income tax system: allow a portion of your earnings to be tax-free in order to maintain a sufficient standard of living.

Those who complain that the flat tax isn't progressive are mistaken. Just look at the effective tax rates in the Flat Tax Rate Table.

The flat tax eliminates all double-taxation on personal savings, dividends, and capital gains. This is especially good news for retirees. Dividends and interest payments would not be taxable because the tax on profits has already been *paid at the corporate level* and because interest payments would no longer be tax-deductible for corporations.

Retirement benefits—whether from Social Security, (don't forget, you already paid taxes on those contributions to Social Security during your working years) annuities or other retirement vehicles funded with after-tax dollars, or cash values from life insurance policies that exceed paid premiums—would no longer be subject to tax.[2] Right now the system penalizes people who choose to save rather than spend what they earn. Dividends are taxed on both the corporate and individual levels. This amounts to double or triple taxation.

By sweeping away savings, dividends, and capital gains taxes, the flat tax will create more capital and greater incentives for risk-takers. That would mean, over time, more savings and investments—leading to greater economic growth and a higher standard of living.

The flat tax would increase returns on capital. People would have the incentive to invest more. In addition, the value of investment assets would be boosted by the flat tax's benign rates. Just look at what happened when the capital gains tax for primary residential housing was substantially eased in 1997: The average value of a house grew significantly faster each year than before the break.

Politicians would no longer be able to give breaks for some types of investments and throw up barriers around others. You would choose how to invest your money—not the pols or tax collectors.

Additional benefits to business from the elimination of dividend taxation are detailed later in this chapter under the Corporate Plan.

Social Security benefits would also become free from taxation under this plan. Right now Social Security recipients face stiff taxes on their benefits if they receive dividends and interest and/or if they continue to work. Retirement should not be a time for the government to take a second bite out of your earnings.

By eliminating double-taxes on savings, the flat tax would help you save for retirement and would let you keep far more of your retirement income.

The flat tax would get rid of the "death" tax once and for all. This horrid levy is supposed to be totally phased out by the year 2010— only to rise again from the dead and be restored in 2011. The flat tax would make repeal of this tax permanent. You should be allowed to provide for your family by passing along the fruits of your labor. By ensuring their welfare, the flat tax will truly allow you to rest in peace. No taxation without respiration.

Killing the death tax would help preserve family businesses when the owner dies instead of forcing a breakup in order to pay the tax bills. By eliminating the death tax, we would encourage the creation of assets instead of the liquidation of capital or wasting money on estate planning, which takes a toll on the allocation of financial resources throughout the economy.

No complicated formulas or abuse from the Alternative Minimum Tax. Millions of American taxpayers must now calculate not only what they owe the IRS in the traditional way but also what they would owe under the Alternative Minimum Tax, which eliminates the benefits

How much money would your family save every year by using the flat tax? (*Year 2006*)

Annual Income	What you owe under the current tax system	Your savings with a 17% flat tax	Tax cut %
30,000	-1,759	-428	24%
35,000	44	-328	100%
40,000	923	-228	25%
50,000	2,423	-28	1%
60,000	4,208	-113	3%
70,000	6,708	-913	14%
80,000	9,458	-1,713	18%
90,000	12,458	-2,513	20%
100,000	15,458	-3,313	21%

What would be your effective tax rate under the flat tax?[*]

Annual Income	Effective Flat Tax Rate
$30,000	-9.2%
$35,000	-5.7%
$40,000	-3.0%
$50,000	1.0%
$60,000	3.7%
$70,000	5.6%
$80,000	7.0%
$90,000	8.1%
$100,000	9.0%
$250,000	14.6%
$500,000	15.8%
$1,000,000	16.4%
$5,000,000 - plus	16.9%

[*] Assumes a married couple with two children under seventeen-years-old claiming the generous exemption of $13,200 for each adult, $4,100 for each child, and the $1,000 child tax credit for each child.

of many deductions. (See chapter three.) Whichever tax liability is highest is the one you owe. They call it the Alternative Minimum Tax, but, as you've seen, the maximum is what you pay.

Under the flat tax, there is no AMT. No bait and switch system of holding out the prospect of deductions only to hit you with an astronomically higher rate. There's one rate, and one rate only.

The flat tax wouldn't be mandatory—you could stick with the old system. For people accustomed to today's tax tyranny, freedom can be a scary prospect. As a result, they focus on the deductions they'll lose—instead of the bottom line—that the flat tax is, above all, a tax cut.

So we give people a choice. They can opt for the new flat tax or they can file under the old system. This type of dual system is being used successfully in Hong Kong. (See chapter six.)

People would be able to see for themselves which is better—the flat tax or the old system. It wouldn't take long for most folks to realize that the new was infinitely better, simpler than the old. They wouldn't have to take my word for it.

This dual system is, essentially, the opposite of today's Alternative Minimum Tax system: whichever tax liability is lowest is the one you'd pay.

THE CORPORATE FLAT TAX PLAN

On the corporate side, the flat tax simplifies life even more dramatically than it does on the personal side.

All profits would be taxed at the rate of 17 percent. Profits are derived by taking a company's total revenue and subtracting 1) wages and salaries, 2) purchases of materials and other inputs necessary to run the business and producing the business's goods and/or services, and 3) purchases of plant and equipment.

The flat tax would dramatically slash the current business tax rate. And it would junk all the rigmarole involving depreciable assets and also close today's loopholes.

Companies could expense all investments—no more depreciation schedules. Currently small businesses can expense only up to

$100,000 a year immediately. Why shouldn't they—and all companies—be allowed to expense *all* investments?

Under a flat tax, depreciation schedules and credits would go into the dumpster. Businesses would be allowed to expense immediately the purchase of long-lived physical assets. If a company bought a piece of machinery, the cost would be written off entirely in the year in which the purchase was made. No more depreciating an asset over a number of years. No more trying to figure out if a particular asset qualifies for some credit or for accelerated depreciation.

If a company made large investments and therefore had negative income during a year, the loss could be carried forward to use against future profits for as many years as necessary to use it up.

This is so good, it bears repeating: Money spent for plant and equipment would offset taxable income and could be carried forward indefinitely to be applied against future years if the cost of the investments more than offsets a company's tax liability.

Allowing entrepreneurs to invest more easily in their businesses will encourage greater investment and help drive economic growth. Companies will base their decisions on what makes good business sense instead of tax implications.

Some flat tax opponents say immediate expensing of business investments will only produce a replay of the 1980s real estate debacle that occurred after the liberalization of depreciation schedules and other changes. The market subsequently overheated, with real estate tax shelters and overbuilding resulting in a sensational bust. The debacle was a major factor in the Savings and Loan industry collapse that ended up costing taxpayers almost $100 billion.

But critics miss two critical points: First, real estate became "overinvested" because it received far more special breaks than did other industries. Under the flat tax, it would *not* be a favored industry, in terms of taxes. If all sectors received immediate expensing, there'd be no tax code-related incentive to invest in one sector over another, as happened with real estate.

Corporate loopholes, all of them, would be abolished under the flat tax. For example, there'd be no more of those "manufacturing" tax credits for Starbucks or, for that matter, massive free-for-all tax give-aways like the 2004 American Jobs Creation Act detailed in our first chapter.

Interest payment deductions would also be eliminated under the flat tax. In effect, the flat tax, by removing the deadweight of taxation from both borrowers and lenders, would make the credit market more efficient. The cost of lending would decrease, resulting in an advantageous drop in interest rates. (See chapter seven for more details.)

Both limited liability companies (LLCs) and S Corps are compatible with the flat tax. The "purity" of LLCs and S Corporations would be preserved. The flat tax would not levy a double tax on these sorts of businesses and their owners/employees. Instead of passing profits through to shareholders/owners, the flat tax would levy the 17 percent tax on those profits at the business level. Any profits paid to shareholders would be *free* of tax. Thus there would continue to be no double taxation of profits.

The flat tax will let companies increase dividends and benefit shareholders. The tax cut of May 2003 showed the positive effects of lowering the dividend tax on individuals. The maximum personal rate on dividends is now 15 percent; it had previously been 38 percent. As a result, hundreds of companies raised their dividends, and scores of others have instituted them, delighting—and enriching—their stockholders. The decrease in the dividend tax prompted Microsoft in late 2004 to reward its stockholders special windfall of some $30 billion.

If just a reduction in the dividend tax could do this much, imagine the benefits to be unleashed if the tax was eliminated, as would occur under the flat tax.

The flat tax would encourage greater transparency. Every year corporations avoid more than $18 billion in taxes because the current code is so fraught with complex rules governing all sorts of write-offs.[3]

With its straightforward rules about what constitutes profits and what can be deducted, the flat tax leaves no room for creative accounting. Immediate business investment write-offs and low tax rates provide little opportunity for the elaborate tax avoidance schemes.

Killing the dividend tax would also help corporate governance. The tax on dividends has traditionally encouraged corporations to hold on to profits instead of paying most of them out to shareholders. Why give dividends when most of the money is going to end up in the hands of the IRS?

Under a flat tax, companies would have to make a case for keeping profits and not paying them out to shareholders. Management would become more accountable, and there would be far less opportunity for management to fritter away retained earnings that should otherwise go to stockholders.

The flat tax will only tax companies on the income they make in the United States. Today multinational corporations are subject to U.S. taxes on income that they earn overseas. They pay taxes to the country in which they operate *and then* they're liable for any difference between the rate they paid abroad and the 35 percent U.S. rate. Such tax policy ensures that no matter where a U.S. company makes a profit, it will pay the 35 percent tax when all is said and done. Unless of course, the company leaves the money overseas—then the tax is usually deferred. Which is why, as I discuss later, Congress in 2004 gave companies a temporary tax break if they brought those profits to the U.S. They might even pay more if the foreign government has a higher corporate tax rate than we have in America. Unfortunately, the United States has one of the world's highest corporate tax rates, so this is mostly a theoretical problem.

Consequently, U.S. business faces an unfair disadvantage: competing against companies from nations such as France and the Netherlands that are only taxed within their borders and keep a larger percentage of earnings because they don't face two tax bills.

By taxing U.S. companies only on what they make in the United States, the flat tax removes a key hurdle for American international business, allowing more effective competition abroad.

The flat tax would create a more receptive environment to free-market benefit plans. As things now stand, many companies are already cutting back on fringe benefits, especially those regarding health care. They are either dropping company plans altogether or are forcing employees to increase the share they pay for health insurance premiums (so-called co-pays) and raising their deductibles.

As daily headlines make clear, traditional corporate pension plans are anything but secure. Look at the travails of many of our airlines' personnel. Countless steel workers have also seen promised pensions either reduced or vaporized altogether. The Pension Benefit Guarantee Corporation, the federal agency that insures corporate pension plans, is now in the red and may itself collapse if it is not bailed out by Congress.

Consequently, companies are moving away from so-called defined benefit pension plans—those in which pensioners receive a fixed amount each month depending their years of service and salary history. They're increasingly offering defined contribution plans such as 401(k)s. In defined contribution plans, money is put into a worker's account, and it grows tax-free. The payout depends on how much the account actually grows during the person's working years and the age at which the worker decides to make withdrawals.

The Bush administration has proposed several reforms here, including a tough provision to force companies over seven years to pay off the unfunded liabilities of their defined-benefit pension plans

There would be no deductions for fringe benefits under the Flat Tax. Since the corporate profits tax would drop from 35 percent to 17 percent, the actual loss to businesses would be minimal. In fact, to retain employees, many companies would still offer fringe benefits—or raise workers' pay.

Under the Flat Tax, 401(k)-type and HSA-type plans would flourish as never before. The nice thing about such plans is that *you* own them—not the employer, the Washington politicians, the union, or some set of employer- or union-appointed trustees.

The Numbers Show: The Flat Tax Will Create Wealth and Government Revenue

Think of it this way: How many home runs could a Babe Ruth, a Hank Aaron, or a Barry Bonds have hit if their bats had fifty-pound weights attached to them? How many touchdown passes could great quarterbacks, such as John Elway or Joe Montana, have thrown if the footballs had weighed one hundred pounds? Reduce the tax burden on people, and they will produce more. Simplistic analogies? Sure, but absolutely truthful.

Tax-cutter John F. Kennedy was right: A rising tide does indeed lift all boats.

From 2005 to 2015 the flat tax would generate $56 billion more in net government income tax revenue than the current tax code, according to Fiscal Associates, whose forecasts are based on the method, in increasing use today, of dynamic analysis.

Dynamic analysis more effectively measures the effects of tax cutting; how increased incentives for more productive work and additional risk-taking lead to the creation of greater wealth. Because it is based on a real-world understanding of the economy and human behavior, the technique is gaining favor over so-called "static analysis" used by the government to assess the impact of tax law changes. (The differences between dynamic and static analysis will be explored later.)

According to Fiscal Associates, wealth producing effects of the flat tax would begin immediately: higher returns on investment will trigger more investing, increasing the value of equities and other assets, such as housing. After an initial four-year transition period, during which tax receipts would be lower than under our current system, this activity will translate into soaring government revenues.

An estimated $6 trillion in additional assets would be created as a result of the flat tax—an immense boost to our nation's balance sheet.

As you can see in the chart below, a flat tax enacted in 2005 would, four years from now, produce $11 billion more for the government than the current system.

Economic theory? No way. Tax reduction bolsters government tax collections by stimulating the creation of wealth. It's similar to investing principles: five percent interest on $10,000 will yield $500 a year; whereas the same interest rate on $20,000 yields $1,000 each year.

More wealth creates more revenue. The same is true for the economy as a whole.

Fiscal Associates finds that the flat tax invigorates the United States economy, particularly in the earlier stages of its enactment. As you can see from the previous table, forecasts of growth under the flat tax dramatically outpace growth we'd get under the current code. These larger initial increases in are the result of capital and investment growth. By

Comparison of Projected Flat Tax Revenue vs. Current Tax Code Revenue

	2005	2006	2007	2008	2009	2010	2011	2012	2013	2014
Flat tax revenue	2,032	2,185	2,337	2,489	2,646	2,806	2,909	3,093	3,258	3,431
CBO target tax revenue	2,096	2,225	2,357	2,497	2,635	2,796	2,887	3,067	3,226	3,393
Net Revenue Effect of Plan	-64	-41	-20	-8	11	11	22	25	32	39

Comparison of Projected Economic Growth Under the Flat Tax vs. Current Tax Code

Economic growth	2005	2006	2007	2008	2009	2010	2011	2012	2013	2014	2015
Current tax code growth forecast	3.8%	3.7%	3.7%	3.4%	3.1%	2.9%	2.8%	2.7%	2.7%	2.6%	2.5%
Flat tax growth forecast	3.8%	5.7%	5.5%	5.3%	5.1%	4.1%	3.7%	3.1%	3.2%	3.2%	3.1%

2015, our Gross Domestic Product will be $2.4 trillion more than it would have been under the current system.

The independent analysis of the flat tax also predicts that the flat tax will lead to nearly 3.5 million new jobs by 2011 that otherwise would not exist. Creating $6 trillion of assets means creating the new jobs that always accompany the entrepreneurial activity of wealth creation. As the economy expands, new jobs are the result.

As we've seen, higher taxes throughout history, and throughout the world, have discouraged investment and productive work and have hampered economic growth. Conversely, cuts in tax rates reduce the price and burden of productive work, of success, of risk taking.

These tables demonstrate that big cuts in tax rates in the past have stimulated the economy *and* produced more tax revenue.

The Steve Forbes Flat Tax Form	
1. Wages & Salary	
2. Number of adults in family	
3. Number of children in family	
4. a) Deductions for adults (multiply line 2 by $13,200) or	
b) Deductions for head of household ($17,160)	
5. Deductions for dependants (multiply line 3 by $4,000)	
6. Total deductions (line 4 plus line 5)	
7. Taxable income (line 1 minus line 7)	
8. Pre-credit tax (multiply line 7 by 17%)	
9. Child tax credit ($1,000 per child under 16)	
10. Earned income tax credit (see EITC rules)	
11. Total tax credits (line 9 plus line 10)	
12. Total tax (line 8 minus line 11)	

In much the same way, the tax cut from a flat tax will stimulate economic activity, the growth and wealth creation that lead to more people making higher incomes that will produce more and not less tax revenue.

Despite all of this evidence, flat tax opponents underestimate the impact that the tax cut resulting from the flat tax will have. Why? One reason is that the connection between risk-taking and economic growth taking is woefully underappreciated by too many economists.

Consider this: Tax receipts from capital gains realizations come to around 4 percent of the federal budget. Capital for startups is but a small percentage of our pool of capital. As a result, conventional economic models miss how vital risk taking is for future prosperity.

They fail to take into account the concept that the Microsofts of tomorrow start as small companies. By definition, startups are small. Microsoft's sales in 1985 were $140 million vs. almost $37 billion in 2004.

Thus, experts tend to underplay the impact the flat tax would have by eliminating the capital gains tax.

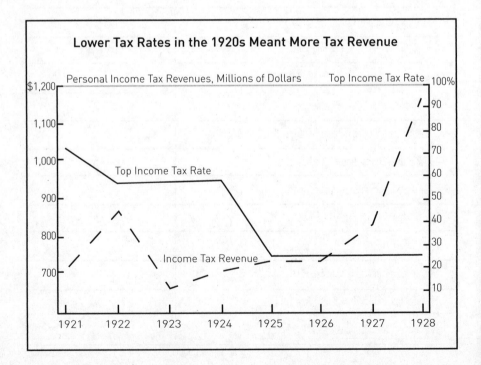

Lower Tax Rates in the 1920s Meant More Tax Revenue

Personal Income Tax Revenues, Millions of Dollars   Top Income Tax Rate

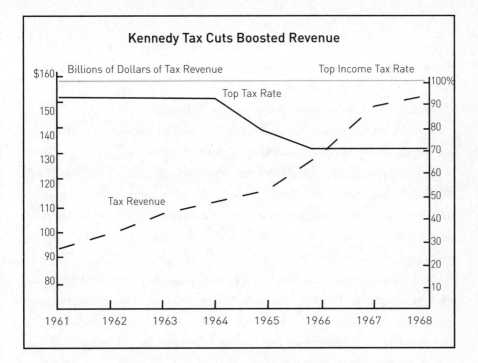

Kennedy Tax Cuts Boosted Revenue

Billions of Dollars of Tax Revenue   Top Income Tax Rate

Top Tax Rate

Tax Revenue

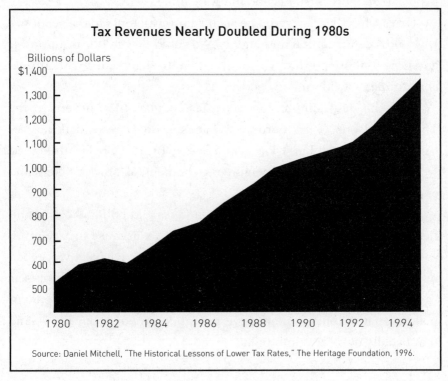

Tax Revenues Nearly Doubled During 1980s

Billions of Dollars

Source: Daniel Mitchell, "The Historical Lessons of Lower Tax Rates," The Heritage Foundation, 1996.

There's another blind spot as well: the way many people are taught economics. Economics is the study of people creating products and services for themselves and other people. Contrary to what most people are taught, it is not about abstractions, such as "allocating scarce resources" or "determining aggregate demand."

Rather, economics is truly about the *creation* of resources, the fantastic process of turning scarcity into abundance. It is about inventors and entrepreneurs coming up with products and services that create demand: How risk-taker Henry Ford's assembly lines turned the automobile, once a toy for the rich, into a necessity every working person could afford. Or how Steve Jobs's wonderful innovation—the iPod— grew into a whole new industry.

Too many people have been taught—and now believe—that economics is simply about the "allocation of scarce resources." They don't understand that wealth begets wealth: Ever more powerful, versatile chips gave rise to the iPod, for example; the automobile increased mobility, enabling people to do more business and innovate more easily.

That's why a flat tax would be such a powerful tonic to the economy. It would free up capital and energy. We could devote our brainpower and time to more productive pursuits than trying to cope with a time-consuming, bewildering tax code.

Reducing and simplifying tax rates reduces the burden on the Thomas Edisons, Henry Fords, Steve Jobses, Bill Gateses, Jeff Bezoses (Amazon.com), and Larry Pages and Sergey Brins (Google.com) of the world. Flowers bloom in a benign environment, as do risk-takers and entrepreneurs.

Unfortunately some within the economics and political communities are blind to the likely impact of the flat tax because they're influenced by Washington mindset with its bureaucratic perspective. A good bureaucracy tends to advocate policies that encourage its self-preservation and, better still, its expansion. So there's the tendency to favor policies that encourage more government control over our lives—and that usually translates into higher taxes.

Because of this mindset, Congress is usually wrong when trying to gauge the impact of tax legislation on the economy. Legislators—and our Treasury Department—incorrectly analyze the likely impact of taxes. They rely all-too-readily on so-called "static" analysis that erroneously assumes changes in tax laws have little or no effect on people's behavior.

Can we afford a flat tax system? As this chapter has demonstrated, we can. Indeed, we can't afford not to adopt one. The flat tax would, among other virtues, substantially increase the return on investments and savings. By doing so, it would go hand-in-hand with the creation of personal savings accounts as a way of saving the Social Security system, which has unfunded liabilities in excess of $10 trillion, for younger people.

Even tax lawyers, accountants, and tax-collecting agents would benefit from a more thriving, more opportunity-rich economy. In the ensuing boom, they would find they could apply their talents to more productive pursuits. Heck, even though I'm a conservative, I'd gladly support the creation of one more federal program: job re-training for ex-IRS agents and ex-tax lobbyists.

And how do we prevent the Washington politicians from cluttering up and corrupting the code again? One line of defense is the flat tax's

A movement is afoot that will allow workers to own directly more of their fringe benefits—primarily health care and pensions. With a 401(k), for instance, the employee owns the plan. If she leaves the company, it goes with her. She can easily roll her money over into a new IRA or, if she wishes in many cases, just leave in the existing 401(k). Either way, her plan is separate from the company. Her payout is not dependent on the company's financial health. We see the beginnings of a similar situation with healthcare. Health Savings Accounts (HSAs) are similar to 401(k)s and IRAs in that the worker owns the account and can take it with her if she changes jobs.

very simplicity. All of us can see if the politicians try to change it—no 9 million-word jungle and underbrush to hide new amendments.

Another: require a super-majority vote in Congress—60 percent or two-thirds—to change the flat tax. Most of the big tax increases enacted by Congress over the past 20 years passed with majorities well under 60 percent.

CHAPTER FIVE

Why the Flat Tax Beats a National Retail Sales Tax

The flat tax is not the only solution that has been proposed to address the problem of our monstrous federal income tax code. Another proposal under discussion is the national retail sales tax (NRST). The NRST would be a consumption tax levied at the national level. One variation that has gained a lot of support in Congress is a 30 percent tax on most consumer purchases of goods and services.[1]

The flat tax is a better idea than the NRST for a multiplicity of reasons we will get to shortly. But it should be stressed that supporters of a sales tax have their hearts in the right place—they rightfully believe that what we have today is an abomination, that we are overtaxed and that we are all subject to abuse from the IRS. A sales tax would be infinitely preferable to the current monstrosity. I believe, though, the flat tax is preferable, not least because it could more easily, readily be enacted than a national sales tax: Before a sales tax is put in place, we must first repeal the Sixteenth Amendment to the Constitution, which allows Washington to impose the income tax. Otherwise we will end up with the situation that exists in most states – and indeed in most other countries – and that is both an income tax and a sales tax (or in other countries the Value Added Tax).

First, a little background.

The national retail sales tax is intended to replace personal and corporate income taxes as well as payroll taxes, capital gains levies, and estate and gift taxes. It would be collected on the sale of new goods and services and exempt from all transactions of used items. Business-to-business purchases would also be exempt from taxation.

2004 National Retail Sales Tax Rebate Calculation for the 48 Contingent Stat

Family Size	HHS Annual Poverty Level	Fair Tax Annual Consumption Allowance (single person)	Annual Rebate (single person)
1	$9,310	$9,310	$2,141
2	$12,490	$12,490	$2,873
3	$15,670	$15,670	$3,604
4	$18,850	$18,850	$4,336
5	$22,030	$22,030	$5,067
6	$25,210	$25,210	$5,798
7	$28,390	$28,390	$6,530
8	$31,570	$31,570	$7,261

Potential snags are immediately obvious: What is the definition of new? What constitutes a business? Let's say you sell stuff on eBay; one can imagine people justifying a sales-tax exemption on a slew of items that may or may not really qualify.

The national sales tax plan calls for a refund from Washington for all taxpayers. This refund would be issued each month to offset the tax levied on necessities such as food, clothing, and shelter.

The official poverty level for a family of four is $18,850—the rebate, if this family included a married couple—would be $479 a month or $5,745 a year (see below).

Advocates of the plan say that it would be a progressive tax because it is based on how much a person actually spent.

On the surface, a sales tax can look appealing. It employs some of the same principles that make the flat tax work. It does not create unnecessary and distorted incentives for certain segments of the economy. It

Monthy Rebate (single person)	Fair Tax Annual Consumption Allowance (married couple)	Annual Rebate (married couple)	Monthly Rebate (married couple)
$178	N/A	N/A	N/A
$239	$18,620	$4,283	$357
$300	$21,800	$5,014	$418
$361	$24,980	$5,745	$479
$422	$28,160	$6,477	$540
$483	$31,340	$7,208	$601
$544	$34,520	$7,940	$662
$605	$37,700	$8,671	$723

treats savings and investment neutrally. But, alas, the concept presents numerous challenges:

A national retail sales tax will raise the price of many goods and services. The price of non-exempt goods and services purchased at retail would increase 30 percent.

Partisans reply that such hikes would be overcome by people having higher take-home pay—no more deductions for incomes taxes or FICA taxes. They also insist that the sales tax would sufficiently lower the cost of most goods and services over the long term, so that the 30 percent surcharge would not be noticeable.

According to their reasoning, companies no longer liable for income and federal payroll taxes would have lower costs and could charge less. So they say, the sales tax would not mean massive price increases.

Really? We have to admit we're skeptical. Have you ever heard of a tax—one that's, in effect, a surcharge—making a product less expensive?

Even if sales tax advocates are right, such adjustments take time. Many people may find it hard to believe that employers will raise employee salaries after being freed from having to pay payroll taxes. Competition may make some of it happen. But in the meantime, most people won't believe such a thing will come to pass.

People may also express a similar uncertainty about some features of the flat tax, such as how it will enable taxpayers to come out ahead after losing various deductions. But the difference is that, under that plan, people will have a choice: stick with the old system or try the new. Choice is not an option under a national sales tax system.

The plan's fixed rebates favor those who live in low-cost areas. Those who live in high cost of living cities might receive higher wages, but at the same time they spend more of their money.

Consequently a carpenter living in a metro area like San Francisco would receive a rebate that was smaller in proportion to his income than his counterpart living in a low-cost-of-living region like Mississippi.

Rebates don't correspond to income. No matter how much money you make, you'd still get the same rebate in the mail each month. Poor taxpayers might resent that their well-off counterparts are getting the very same amount they are.

The plan opens the door to encroaching entitlements. There's also the danger that the rebate under the national retail sales tax would morph into something resembling a traditional government entitlement. There would be political pressure to increase the rebates and to then differentiate between people of various incomes.

Do we want to enact something like the NRST that would still force us to maintain massive government spending and a none-too-small bureaucracy? In the final analysis, the rebate would become a de facto entitlement program.

Putting the program in place would mean a new, high cost bureaucracy. A national retail sales tax would require establishing a dedicated government bureaucracy tasked with implementing the rebate program—with its various processes of taxpayer registration and verification, not to mention the payment system itself, generating layers of government paperwork. The cost of such a rebate program would be as much as $500 billion dollars.[2] NRST advocates confirm that the rebate program would add 10 percent to 13 percent to the base sales tax rate. The IRS monster would eventually be reborn.

The NRST would devastate the market for new homes. By taxing new homes at 30 percent, the NRST would constitute a significant disincentive for new home buyers, who are key drivers of economic growth. People would seek to avoid the tax by purchasing existing homes.

Competing with a used-housing market that featured prices 25 percent or more lower than new housing would devastate builders across the nation. Many would be forced out of business.

NRST proponents point out that eventually the prices of new homes would come down and old ones go up. They fail to account for the shock this would bring to the housing market before stabilization occurs.

The tax would raise the already soaring cost of college tuition by 30 percent. College tuition, whose sky-high price is already straining the resources of most families, would be among the goods and services to be taxed by the NRST. There is no way any parent facing college tuitions would want to see a national sales tax enacted.

The NRST would stifle the online industry. The Internet owes its growth, in part, to its status as a little regulated, tax-free zone. The national retail sales tax would stifle this industry with its comprehensive tax blanket covering both goods and services. Goods sold over the Net are not liable to sales tax if the buyer does not live in a state where the seller has a physical presence. A nationwide sales tax would, by definition, tax consumer transactions on the Internet. There would be no more tax-free purchases via Amazon.com

The tax is unfair in times of recession. In a down economy, when you may be earning less, you'd still be hit with the 30 percent tax when purchasing goods and services. Though you may be spending less, a certain portion of these expenditures, such as for your mortgage and other essentials, remains fixed. You'd still have to pay a 30 percent tax on them at a time when you might not be able to afford it. In contrast, the flat tax is based on how much you earn. If you're making less in a bad down economy, you pay less tax. It's a more flexible, accommodating system.

The plan encourages redundant, inappropriate taxation of business. When a company buys, say, a sheet of steel to make a product, it is not supposed to pay sales tax on that material; yet many small outfits end up mistakenly paying anyway. Forty percent of state sales taxes improperly fall on business inputs, according to testimony by Robert Strauss, professor of Economics and Public Policy at Carnegie Mellon

University, before the House Ways & Means Subcommittee on Oversight.[3] This extra unfair layer of taxation reduces a business's profits.

Many fear this unfortunate phenomenon of so-called cascading taxation will be exacerbated by national sales tax. Retail outlets will collect it erroneously, just as they currently do at the state level. Businesses will be even more unfairly taxed.

Collecting the tax using existing state apparatus, as some advocates propose, may not work. Each state has distinctions in what can be taxed. In some states groceries are taxed; in others, they are not. Some states tax newspapers and magazines; in other states these items are exempt. Some states tax clothes; others do not.

Introducing a national sales tax is not a matter of piggybacking on preexisting sales tax systems. It would require a unique, uniform system across all fifty states.

Sales taxes increase tax evasion. Experience shows that sales taxes face major enforcement problems when rates go beyond 10 percent. Studies have concluded that when governments attempt to enforce a retail sales tax at the level proposed with the NRST—30 percent—evasion picks up dramatically. Enforcement becomes a battle against sophisticated avoidance tactics. According to the Organization for Economic Co-operation and Development, "Governments have gone on record as saying a retail sales tax of more than 10 percent to 12 percent is too fragile to tax evasion possibilities..."[4]

The plan's business exemption will encourage tax avoidance. You'll see a rush of eligible and ineligible people seeking to declare themselves "businesses" in order to qualify for the NRST's business exemption. Licenses and exemption certificates for phony businesses would be rampant.

The national retail sales tax puts retailers in the unfair position of policing their customers. Retailers would have to determine, for example, whether the lumber a customer just bought is really meant for business resale—or for fixing up the customer's kitchen. "It is not in the best economic interest of retailers to be especially suspicious of exemptions; questions may cause loss of a profitable sale, and only the government gains when the questions are asked,"[5] writes John Mikesell in *Tax Notes*.

Yes, the NRST would penalize cheating, but that only would affect those who were caught. The best solutions to tax evasion are preventive, not merely punitive. And the NRST only offers a punitive approach.

The number of taxpayers would increase under the NRST. Right now an estimated 58 million income-earning households pay either no income taxes or have a "negative" tax, which occurs when the government refunds an amount that exceeds the income tax, as is the case with the Earned Income Tax Credit. Those 58 million households translate into about 122 million Americans. Those zero-income-tax households would be added to the tax rolls under a national retail sales tax. More people would pay tax under the NRST than even under the current system. In contrast, the flat tax removes millions of households from the tax rolls.

The NRST would unnecessarily inflate the cost of government to you, the taxpayer. The National Retail Sales Tax would also apply to purchases made by the government. The Pentagon, for instance, would even pay a 30 percent levy on the cost of an aircraft carrier. Think of all the supplies and equipment Uncle Sam buys. The tax would raise the cost of government in America by literally hundreds of billions of dollars. Who would ultimately foot this spiraling bill? You, the taxpayer—possibly in the form of an even higher tax rate. Some experts say that the national sales tax rate would have to rise to about 60 percent in order to account for the combined effects of higher cost of government and evasion tactics.[6]

Governments—federal, state , and local—don't pay sales taxes now and aren't likely to pay a national sales tax. Which means that the rest of us will likely foot the bill for that shortfall.

Political obstacles to the NRST may be too great. Passing the NRST would require a huge mobilization of political resources—far greater than those needed to pass a simple flat tax.

To work as intended, the national sales tax would require the repeal of the Sixteenth Amendment, which would be difficult and time-consuming. It would require the approval by a two-thirds vote of both houses of Congress. Then the amendment would have to be approved by thirty-eight states. This formidable task is why we have had so few amendments to the Constitution.

With all these drawbacks, the national retail sales tax is opposed by some of the nation's most prominent tax experts. They include former Congressman Dick Armey and Grover Norquist, the president of Americans for Tax Reform, who have publicly opposed the NRST's passage and support a flat tax.

The NRST nonetheless has endorsements from many Representatives in Congress and a number of U.S. senators—but not necessarily from their constituents.

Consider the cautionary tale of Republican Senator Jim DeMint of South Carolina, who recently won the seat of retiring Senator Fritz Hollings. During his campaign, DeMint advocated the national retail sales tax. It cost him vital support. DeMint's opponent's consistent attacks on this issue eroded DeMint's huge lead and he had to do some fancy footwork to stop the hemorrhaging before eventually winning the election. Republicans lost a Senate battle in Louisiana in 1996 because the Democrat—current incumbent Mary Landrieu—was able to successfully demagogue against the Republican for supporting a national retail sales tax.

Aside from these episodes, however, the sales tax has not come under the national scrutiny that the flat tax has endured. In contrast, the flat tax has been tested in the flames of the public square. It has been hit with numerous, oft-misleading attacks. Yet it continues to garner support.

A flat tax would bypass or address all the previously mentioned pitfalls of a national sales tax. It would need no constitutional amendment—just one simple law to provide the solution to today's unfair Byzantine tax code.

A flat tax has all the principle benefits of a national sales tax without its chief liability: enforcement and evasion difficulties.

A flat tax would be fairer and simpler than a national sales tax. Under a flat tax, for example, everyone would get the same exemptions. It would also be more efficient, because there's a system already in place that is a proven tool in collecting the huge amounts of revenue.

It's not that the national sales tax is all bad. It's just that we can reform the current code faster, and better, with a flat tax.

CHAPTER SIX

Other Nations Are Already Succeeding with the Flat Tax

President Bush's call for major tax reform may finally provide the U.S. with a serious opportunity to enact the flat tax. If we do, we'll follow the lead of a growing number of countries, large and small, that have either instituted or are moving towards adopting a flat tax. Nations that already have one include Russia, Hong Kong, Romania, Lithuania, and Slovakia, among quite a few others. The concept, meanwhile, is under consideration in China, Germany, Spain, Croatia, and other countries.

We should understand why the flat tax idea is rapidly spreading. It helps create more prosperity, and countries increasingly recognize that if they don't adopt the flat tax, they will lose jobs, capital, and their own ambitious entrepreneurs to more growth-friendly nations. In other words, just as competition is essential for economic progress, so too tax competition spurs more growth and opportunity. The late, great banker Walter Wriston never tired of observing that capital—money and people—goes where it is welcome and stays where it is well treated.

In the U.S., the flat tax is perceived as a radical idea. But in countries around the world, it is known as a powerful tool that, in a short time, has helped turn around struggling economies and usher in growth and prosperity.

In Romania, the mayor of Bucharest, Trajan Basecu, won a stunning upset victory for that country's presidency in December 2004 by promising to replace the old, complicated tax code with a simple, 16 percent flat tax. Soon after taking office, Basecu did just that. By the start of 2005, Romania was enjoying a flat tax, with a 16 percent rate on both personal incomes and business profits.

The Russians revolutionized their tax system in 2001 with a flat-rate solution, and many other Central and Eastern European nations have done the same. Latvia, Estonia, and Lithuania have proven the flat tax's validity for more than a decade. Two small British entities, the Channel Islands of Jersey and Guernsey, have long been flat-tax success stories. Hong Kong, formerly part of China but still maintaining its own unique tax code, has built its income tax around an effective hybrid of the flat tax for almost sixty years.

Meanwhile even Spain (with its socialist, anti-American government) is considering a 30 percent flat tax. The rate is high by flat tax standards—which is what you might expect from Western European leftists. But at least they see the virtue of simplicity.

These countries realize that a flat tax establishes a simple and low-rate system that provides powerful and enormous incentives for economic growth. It spares taxpayers the countless headaches of complying with incomprehensible, corrupt tax codes. Amazingly, communists and ex-communists seem to have gotten the message faster than we capitalists.

A closer look at the experience of these nations provides a window on the possibilities offered by the flat tax.

RUSSIA: THE BEGINNINGS OF REAL REFORM

Before enacting a flat tax, Russia had a tax system that made America's tax beast look tame by comparison. The predecessor of today's Russian flat tax was a system designed in hell. Under communism, getting ahead was synonymous with cheating. The tax system drawn up in the aftermath of the fall of communism reflected a confused understanding of what free enterprise and the rule of law were all about.

Russia's system contained so many different taxes that ordinary citizens trying to comply with each and every one found themselves working fulltime as their own tax specialists. These taxes included four different Social Security taxes, layered on top of marginal income tax rates of up to 30 percent, value added taxes, excise taxes, housing taxes, and death taxes.

All these were further complicated by confusing levels of regional and local taxes that invariably overlapped.[1] Russia's tax system was really one of institutionalized chaos. Tax compliance meant wrestling with different tax-collecting agencies and attempting to navigate each agency's perspective payment calendar and fiscal year. To call taxation in Russia a nightmare was a gross understatement.

As a result of this labyrinth, corruption became endemic. Most Russians viewed the government with suspicion. In a nation that has a legacy of more than seventy years of routinely lying and proclaiming phony output numbers, it was no surprise that—in the face of bewildering, onerous exactions—most people hid or underreported their incomes. After all, in the former Soviet Union, even workplace productivity was a sham. "They pretend to pay us, we pretend to work," was the bitter joke among Soviet citizens during the Communist era.

Overlapping taxes and haphazard, oft-venal enforcement hardly helped to increase their level of confidence. Taxpayers assumed there would be quarterly changes to the tax code. Tax-collecting officials became notorious for negotiating tax liabilities instead of determining them based on a tax statute. When a tax regime becomes so convoluted that tax collecting has a legal component of arbitrariness, it cultivates corruption, evasion, and, ultimately, failure.

A classic example of the old Russian tax code's built-in corruption and evasion was its reclassifying wages as "interest." This practice amounted to employees' receiving a loan from their employer, which they "reinvested" by depositing it for a super-high rate of interest, often several hundred percent. The difference between the loan interest and the deposit interest became their wages—except these wages were exempt from payroll taxes and subject to little or no income tax. As in so many nations, Russia's tax code funneled brain power into shady tax avoidance.

Not surprisingly, the Russian government saw tax collections fall in the 1990s. Personal tax revenues experienced a huge decline. More than 60 percent of individual income taxes went completely uncollected because the code was so contorted, so conducive to endless shakedowns and payoffs, not to mention outright violence.[2]

The International Monetary Fund (IMF) is an agency that is supposed to help troubled economies. Instead it has damaged them for decades with anti-growth, pro-inflation policy prescriptions that can only be described as clueless. Like America's State and Treasury Departments, the IMF has long operated under the misconception that you increase government revenue by raising taxes. The agency was—and is—usually oblivious to the truth that lower, simple rates would do wonders in reviving moribund economies.

The agency, typically, exacerbated the confusion: Under pressure from the IMF, income taxes were, astoundingly, not lowered but *raised*.

The move compounded Russian taxpayers' misery.

Small wonder the Russian economy contracted. The IMF-inspired tax hike not only failed to fill government coffers, but also helped to precipitate an economic collapse in 1998.

Massive stealing also played a role. Most of the billions of dollars the IMF pumped into the Russian government ended up in private overseas bank accounts. Inflationary monetary policy also didn't help. The oppressive tax laws and corrupt oligarchy worked to bring about the collapse of the ruble and the spectacular implosion of Russian markets.

REAL REFORM

It looked as if a free market might never take root in this former Soviet nation. Still, Russia's acute crisis brought about one positive development: the realization that something needed to be done. The situation could not continue.

President Vladimir Putin, who took office in 2000, enacted reforms that have moved the country toward economic recovery and sustained growth. Putin inherited an awful legacy. Under his predecessor, Boris Yeltsin, a handful of rich, powerful individuals systematically robbed the rest of the country. These oligarchs turned privatization into a gimmick for looting government assets. They bought mineral-rich and asset-rich companies at a fraction of their true worth. Their acts were a communist caricature of capitalism in action—a clique of rapacious plutocrats ruthlessly exploiting everyone else.

Putin and his economic advisors pushed for what they saw as the best option to help their economy grow and to combat the spread of black market forces—a simple flat-rate income tax. They also enacted what was, for Russia, a revolution—the beginnings of genuine property rights law.

In July 2000, only months after taking office, Putin's government pushed through the Duma a 13 percent flat tax on personal incomes that went into effect on January 1, 2001. The result: higher tax revenues collected every year since.

In the first year of the flat tax, the Russian government's collection of personal income taxes increased 25 percent, after accounting for inflation. Again in 2002, government receipts rose almost 25 percent (denominated in real dollars) over 2001.

By the end of 2004, government revenues from income taxes had more than doubled over the four years the flat tax had been on the books.[3]

Russia's experience refutes flat-tax skeptics who think such a system would cost the government money. Besides the flat tax bringing in more rubles, those revenues also increased proportionately—from 12 percent of government revenues to 17 percent.[4]

I must confess to feeling more than a little wry amusement when the *New York Times*, which vociferously trashed the flat tax proposed by

Russian Income Tax Collections: 2001–2004

Year	2001	2002	2003	2004
Rubles (billions)	255.5	357.1	449.8	574.1
Nominal increase	46.7%	39.7%	27.2%	26.1%
Real increase	25.2%	24.6%	15.2%	14.4%

Source: Alvin Rabushka, *The Flat Tax at Work in Russia: Year Four, January–June*, January 26, 2005.

Yours Truly while running for president, hailed President Putin for his initiatives. In an editorial titled "Russia's Promising Tax Plan," the paper praised him for "radically simplifying the code and slashing rates."

A couple of years ago, on a visit to the U.S., the Russian president met with American business executives at the New York Stock Exchange. He was to see President Bush the following day. I asked Putin if he was going to persuade the president to push for a flat tax in America. As you'd expect, he diplomatically ducked that question and replied by boasting about tax reforms in Russia. "We now have the lowest personal income tax rate in Europe (since surpassed by Georgia, which has a 12 percent rate vs. Russia's 13 percent). We are going to reduce again the corporate tax rate. My budget experts don't like this, but we may also reduce the value added tax. These reductions will make our economy stronger."

Putin knew what he was doing. He later lowered the corporate tax from 30 percent to 24 percent; Russia's VAT of 20 percent, however, remains unchanged.

My flat tax proposal has a rate of 17 percent. Putin instituted a 13 percent rate. I never thought the day would come when a former communist and KGB agent such as Vladimir Putin would be more radical on taxes than I.

Putin's reforms were publicly sold to taxpayers as the "bargain" they were. The government actually marketed the flat tax with commercials. It pointed out how much lower the new rate was in comparison with the old tax system. Prosperity and success would no longer be treated as tax-punishable crimes.

It is true that other factors, such as high oil prices, have also played a role in Russia's recent economic growth. President Putin also enacted other economic reforms, such as the start of property rights. But the flat tax has been vitally important in building an economic foundation that should help Russia's prosperity continue.

This, of course, raises the fundamental question: Can Russia make a truly successful transition to a free-market, rule-of-law, Western-style democracy?

President Putin's moves on tax simplification and property rights were heartening steps. Certainly the first editor of *Forbes* Magazine's Russian edition, Paul Klebnikov, who was gunned down in July 2004 by contract murderers, thought he saw the beginning of grassroots, modernizing forces. But the fact that Klebnikov was assassinated—after a series of tough, insightful articles on Russia's corrupt oligarchs—makes one wonder about Russia's future.

If kept in place, the flat tax and other economic changes will create new middle classes that, eventually, will demand more civil liberties and individual rights. Russia's future rests on such people.

FLAT TAX SUCCESS IN THE BALTICS

In the mid-1990s, the Baltic nations of Estonia, Latvia, and Lithuania emerged from the Soviet era of economic and political repression looking to enact major reforms. Expanding their economies was obviously a top priority (see box). The nations wanted to rid themselves of the corrupt shadow economies that were the results of their former communist systems. Each of these nations has each adopted some form of the flat tax, with dramatic results.

ESTONIA: A MAGNET FOR FOREIGN CAPITAL

Estonia's flat tax reform has helped this small, low-population state emerge from under the dead weight of communism and become, in just a few years, one of the region's most vibrant economies.

In 1994, under the leadership of Prime Minister Mart Laar, Estonia scrapped its old multirate system in favor of a simple flat tax. As part of a larger economic reform package, a 26 percent flat tax was enacted across the board on business and personal incomes. The system allows large (for Estonia) personal exemptions of about $1,000 a year.

The 26 percent rate was fairly high by flat tax standards. But it still worked—so well, in fact, that Estonia recently passed legislation to reduce the rate by 2 percent per year until it drops to 20 percent in 2007. Personal exemptions are scheduled to double to $2,000 over the next two years.

In 2000, the corporate income tax was made even flatter. Businesses were required to pay taxes only on distributed profits. Before, undistributed profits had been taxed, regardless of whether they were plowed back into investments or simply retained as cash by the business.

> The informal economy, also called the gray or shadow economy, exists outside the explicit protection of the rule of law and can result when laws and regulation are perceived as unfairly and excessively constricting routine business practices.
>
> In America we take for granted the fact that you can set up a lawful, new enterprise in a matter of days. In countries where it can take months, if not years, as well as considerable amounts of money, to set up a legal business, a shadow economy will emerge and operate outside of the law. Another spur to informal economies is excessive taxes and suffocating regulations.
>
> Nations with stable laws and legal systems and sensible, reasonable tax codes also have smaller informal "gray" economies. Gray economies are less efficient. Efforts aimed at evading detection reduce a business's ability to be fully productive. Thus, most informal entities have stunted growth potential: Their illegality puts a ceiling of sorts on how big they can become. They don't want to become so sizeable that they attract attention from the authorities. As a result, economic growth is curbed and so are tax receipts.

The results? The flat tax in Estonia—aided by other reforms, including a stable currency—has helped the nation become an international hot spot for foreign investment. With a mere population of about 1.4 million people, Estonia attracted about $890 million in foreign direct investment in 2003 and some $926 million in 2004. Per capita, that's more than ten times what red-hot China is receiving.

Lower taxes and increased investment have helped the economy grow at impressive rates. In the five years preceding the flat tax, Estonia's economy had undergone a crippling contraction. In the eight years following the flat tax's inception, Estonia has had an average growth of 5.2 percent each year, which is particularly noteworthy when compared with the stagnant standards of Western Europe.

Impressively, Estonia ranks number 4 (out of 155 countries) in the Index of Economic Freedom, published by the Heritage Foundation (on whose board I sit) and the *Wall Street Journal*.

LITHUANIA: THE BALTIC TIGER

What kind of economic performance does it take to earn the nickname "Baltic Tiger"? According to *The Economist:* solid government revenues, low inflation and low unemployment. The magazine coined the term in 2003 to reflect the rapid expansion and newfound stability of the Baltic region, particularly in Lithuania.

The post-Soviet era in Lithuania began with highly depressed incomes and rigid market structures. Shifting from a command economy to free markets, Lithuania faced the task of privatizing underperforming government industries. The road, to put it mildly, was rocky. The 1990s was largely a decade of unchecked economic depression—a shrinking economy, raging inflation, and swelling budget deficits. Then, in 1998, Lithuania battled a banking crisis resulting from the shock of the economic collapse of neighboring Russia.

These economic storms prompted Lithuania to enact radical changes, including a flat tax.[5]

Lithuania places a single tax rate on personal incomes—33 percent. That may be high, but it's lower and simpler than it was before.

Corporate profits are taxed at 15 percent. Lithuania allows a personal exemption of about $1,200 a year, and taxpayers can also deduct their contributions to pension funds. Personal real estate is exempt from capital gains, while other capital gains are taxed at 10 percent and business gains at 15 percent.

Lithuania's flat tax permits corporations to reinvest profits tax-free in fixed assets, and in research and development, a policy that encourages businesses to grow. Today Lithuania's booming economy is an astonishing testament to what a fair, flat-tax system can generate: The country had the fastest-growing economy in the Baltics in 2002, 6.7 percent. In 2003, Lithuania's gangbuster growth rate was an eye-popping 9 percent; for 2004 it came in around 8 percent.

This formerly communist nation makes the lesson crystal clear: A flat tax can turn the most backward economy into a smashing success in the course of a few years.

LATVIA: INFLATION PLUMMETS

In the Baltic nation of Latvia, the flat tax, enacted in 1995, proved equally successful. Today personal incomes are taxed at 25 percent, corporate profits at 15 percent. Sales of private real estate are tax-exempt.

In the five years before adopting the flat tax, Latvia, like Lithuania and Estonia, experienced a bone-crushing economic contraction. In the five years after adopting the flat tax, Latvia's economy has been growing at a respectable annual rate of around 4 percent. Inflation, which plagued the economy at 25 percent in 1995, was down to less than 4 percent by 2003.[6]

UKRAINE: FLAT TAX OFFERS HOPE FOR A NEW GOVERNMENT

Before the flat tax was passed, experts estimated that the shadow economy accounted for more than half of Ukraine's economic output—all of which escaped income taxation.[7] Ukraine's parliament passed a 13 percent flat tax on personal incomes, which went into effect in 2004. Under the previous system, which was bewilderingly complicated, income was taxed according to five brackets, with a top rate of 40 percent.

Ukraine's flat tax was passed by huge margins. Like politicians in Russia and the Baltic states before them, the country's legislators grasped the dire straits their economy was in.

At this writing, the system has been in force barely a year. Ukrainian officials expect to bring many individuals and businesses out from the informal shadow economy and finally make them legitimate tax payers. After all, why risk breaking the law when the taxes are now so low and so simple? The expectation is that the new system will increase government revenues despite a big drop in tax rates, as occurred in Russia.

As in Russia, Ukraine's move is intended as part of an even larger tax reform program. To date, Ukraine has lowered its corporate tax rate from 30 percent to 25 percent, and lawmakers plan to reduce the value added tax.

Ukraine has been the center of headline-making political turmoil— a rigged presidential election that sparked an uprising leading to a second election and the victory of a modern, forward-looking, pro-Western reformer. For the economy, these developments couldn't have come at a better time. If the new government pursues and strengthens pro-free-market reforms, then Ukraine will create a new entrepreneurial middle class and prosper like its Baltic neighbors. That, in turn, will bode well for shaking off the country's hideous, Soviet-era inheritance of corruption, stagnation, and oppression. Indeed, Ukraine could become a model for Russian political reformers.

Another potential benefit: a Baltic-style economic boom could begin to lessen the serious divide between western Ukraine, which is more European-oriented—it was once part of Poland—and eastern Ukraine, which has been intimately tied to Russia.

SERBIA: BRAVE NEW PRO-GROWTH INCENTIVES

Serbia's economy became a disastrous mess because of the murderous ethnic conflicts that wracked the Balkans for much of the 1990s. Recognizing that drastic steps had to be taken, Serbia passed a flat tax in 2003 that levies a 14 percent tax on both business and individual incomes. Serbia is also providing a three-year window for companies to take advantage of a new incentive: Companies that invest in underdeveloped areas of Serbia and employ more than 100 workers will be exempt from corporate income tax for 10 years. Serbia also plans to make further cuts in its tax rates. Pro-growth incentives such as this will help turn Serbia into another flat-tax success story in coming years.

ROMANIA: POISED TO BECOME A GLOBAL PLAYER

Romania had levied taxes at five different rates: 18 percent, 23 percent, 28 percent, 34 percent and 40 percent. Prime Minister Tariceanu said the old tax regime only served to hinder the success of business: "The burdening fiscal policy which was in effect has stopped Romanian companies from gaining capital and becoming competitive in foreign markets." The World Bank recently estimated that Romania's gray economy accounted for more than one-third of that nation's economic activity.[8]

Having run on a flat-tax platform, newly-elected President Trajan Basecu, who had been an underdog in the race, moved quickly after his December 12, 2004, victory. By December 29, his new cabinet, headed by Prime Minister Calin Popescu Tariceanu, enacted a 16 percent flat tax on both individual and business income. The tax took effect only days later, on January 1.

Astonishingly, the IMF has praised Romania's flat-tax reform effort as "good fiscal policy." Romanian officials are anticipating increased investment and an expanding economy. As has happened in other countries, the low, simple tax should nudge the nation's hidden entrepreneurs into the open.

Prime Minister Tariceanu believes the flat tax will revolutionize Romania's role in the global economy. As a result of the flat tax, Romania is now poised to enter the global marketplace with a competitive edge.[9]

GEORGIA: THE LOWEST INCOME TAX RATE IN EUROPE

With a very convincing 107-to-11 vote by its parliament on December 22, 2004, Georgia added its name to the long list of nations reforming their tax systems by passing a flat tax. At 12 percent, Georgia now has the lowest income tax rate in Europe. The flat tax replaced its four rates of 12 percent, 15 percent, 17 percent and 20 percent.

This new tax code also lowers the Social Security tax from 33 percent to 20 percent and will lower the VAT to 18 percent (a 2 percent decrease) by July 2005.[10] The Georgian law replaced the entire tax code, reducing its overall size by 95 percent.

SLOVAKIA: "THE DETROIT OF EUROPE"

Much like Russia and the Baltic States, the formerly communist state of Slovakia badly needed to simplify its overly complicated tax code to free itself from the stagnation and corruption of its formerly state-controlled economy.

"Complex" does not begin to describe the shortcomings of Slovakia's former tax code. It had five tax brackets ranging from 10 percent to 38 percent; 90 different exemptions; 19 unique sources of tax-free income; 66 items that were themselves tax-exempt; and an additional 27 items that carried their own particular tax rates.[11] A split value added tax (VAT) taxed some items and services at 14 percent, others at 20 percent, which made the code even more pretzel-like. Confusion reigned because tax laws changed twice a year.

Not surprisingly, countless citizens avoided the tax system altogether. Slovakia's shadow economy accounted for a high percentage of the country's actual economic output. Slovaks had little incentive to create domestic capital because of onerous tax rules. And foreign investment would not come rolling in without reform.

Government leaders knew something had to be done to address this growth-suppressing mess. In October 2003, parliament passed a flat-tax reform bill that was initially vetoed by the president, Rudolph Schuster. Parliament overrode the veto in December. This reform bill unified and simplified the Slovakian tax regime, creating one rate across the board. The personal income tax, the corporate income tax and the VAT, were all set at 19 percent.[12]

Personal income taxes dropped for almost all Slovaks. Those at the high-end of the income scale have seen their highest tax rate fall from

35 percent to 38 percent down to 19 percent. The flat tax avoided a tax increase on lower income taxpayers by including a personal deduction of $2,600; this exempted half the average yearly wage in Slovakia. The previous personal exemption was only $1,246.

The new law reduced the perverse incentives that had driven so much of the economy into the informal sector. As tax rates were slashed and simplified, individuals and businesses began to emerge from the shadows.

The government projected that it would maintain its current level of revenues despite the cuts in tax rates. It did even better: Tax collections soared by 36 percent, shrinking the budget deficit by 93 percent in the first quarter of the new fiscal year.

The country is beginning to see a dramatic increase in foreign direct investment. The *New York Times*, for instance, has dubbed Slovakia the "Detroit of Europe" because of the recent contracts for new facilities for Hyundai–KIA and Peugeot. These agreements will bring billions of dollars of investment to Slovakia for new manufacturing plants that will employ thousands of Slovakians. By attracting businesses with its very competitive tax system, Slovakia hopes to become a beachhead for capitalism's spread across central and eastern Europe.

When international automakers signed billion-dollar agreements to relocate manufacturing facilities to Slovakia, the nation proved it had embarked on the same kind of journey that had transformed Ireland from an economic laggard into the economic dynamo it is today. [See box.]

Remember, taxes are a price. By reducing tax rates, Slovakia rewards and encourages more productive work, risk-taking and success. Slovakia is now enjoying more job creation as its economic growth tops 5 percent a year—a miracle level by western European standards.

Its success in making the transition from communism to free markets is making Slovakia a poster child for economic reform. President Bush, who has pledged to reform the U.S. tax code, publicly praised Prime Minister Mikulas Dzurinda for his reforms. During their February 2005 meeting in Bratislava, Bush, without prompting, made a point of touting the flat tax:

"I complimented the Prime Minister on putting policies in place that have helped this economy grow...the president put a flat tax in place; he simplified his tax code, which has helped to attract capital and create economic vitality and growth. I really congratulate you and your government for making wise decisions."

The Slovaks still smart from being regarded as poor, backward cousins to the Westernized and supposedly more sophisticated Czechs during the days of the Czechoslovakian union. As the Irish did with the English, the Slovaks are determined to turn the tables. Success is indeed the best revenge.

Slovakia has chosen a course of action that will enable it to become a vibrant state in the twenty-first century's global economy. The World Bank ranked Slovakia as the most successful nation among those implementing reforms in 2003. The World Bank's report on "Doing Business in 2005," placed Slovakia among the top twenty nations in the world for ease of doing business.

In drastically lowering taxes, Slovakia and its fellow Baltic states will likely follow in the footsteps of Ireland, which has become the economic model for many central and eastern European counties. Decades ago, Ireland adopted an aggressive corporate tax-reduction policy in order to attract investment and serve as a platform for businesses targeting Continental Europe. Many American companies saw this English-speaking island as an ideal jumping-off point for their business invasion of the rest of Europe. Ireland cut business taxes. In the 1980s, to counteract an economic slide, it cut taxes, especially on personal income, even more. It worked. Ireland earned the nickname "Celtic Tiger" as a result of its ability to attract foreign investment and market itself as a location where corporations could thrive.

Ireland has had a long, troubled history with Britain. However, it has now achieved the best revenge: Ireland's per capita income is higher than that of Great Britain.[13]

THE EU: STIRRINGS OF REFORM

Because of their flat tax reforms, Slovakia and other "transition" nations new to the European Union have become fierce economic competitors. Their success is eliciting accusations of unfair play from established nations. Germany and France are accusing Slovakia and other tax-smart countries of creating tax havens and subsidizing their low taxes with EU aid money.

Yet beneath these accusations are the stirrings of reform. As they call for more equitable "tax harmonization" within the union, Germany, France, and others are ever so slowly inching towards serious consideration of the flat tax.

In Germany, Chancellor Gerhard Schroeder is leading the charge in brow-beating Slovakia, Estonia, Lithuania, and Latvia. Germany's burdensome tax regime smothers economic growth, and its corporate tax rate is twice that of Slovakia. Yet at the same time, forces within the German government, particularly in the finance ministry, are seriously studying the flat tax reform. Moreover, Chancellor Schroeder reluctantly announced that Germany would reduce its corporate tax rates to avoid losing more businesses to neighboring, lower-tax countries.

France is also critical of the low taxes in transition states such as Slovakia. France's former finance minister, Nicolas Sarkozy, hammered eastern and central European nations over their tax cuts while in office. He even proposed eliminating the EU subsidies that support economic development in the new EU members. Sarkozy demanded that if tax cutting EU nations were "rich enough" to avoid sky-high tax rates, then they should not expect EU development money.

Isn't this a little hypocritical? The French, of all people, are masters at attracting foreign investment. The *Wall Street Journal* reported that France offers "a dazzling array of tax benefits" to lure foreign businesses.[14] Yet Paris can't understand that tax reform is also an essential part of the recipe for a vital economy. Instead the country keeps adding more special provisions that further complicate its tax code.

Since France offers specific incentives for foreign investment, why doesn't it just go with across-the-board tax simplification?

While the winds of reform are blowing, Germany and France continue to suffer for their reluctance, to date, to make needed tax reforms. Bureaucracies that think they are dependent on overburdened taxpayers for survival cannot tolerate the competition from agile, adaptive nations like Slovakia or Ireland.

EU bureaucrats in Brussels, prompted by Paris and Berlin, constantly pressure Ireland to substantially raise its taxes. But the Emerald Isle refuses—and enjoys more and more prosperity.[15]

IRAQ: A 15 PERCENT CEILING

Iraq currently has a virtual flat tax. The former Coalition Provisional Authority chief, Paul Bremmer, established a 15 percent ceiling for taxes levied by the provisional government. No one knows if this will turn out to be Iraq's permanent tax system. But if the flat tax remains in place, Iraq's chances of achieving real economic growth—something badly needed in the blighted Middle East—will improve immeasurably.

THE CHANNEL ISLANDS: DECADES OF FLAT TAX SUCCESS

In 1940, Jersey enacted a 20 percent flat tax on both individuals and corporations. Its neighbor, Guernsey, did the same 20 years later. Both systems provide generous deductions for adults, children, and dependent relatives.

As the Adam Smith Institute recently reported:

Since the introduction of the flat tax, the economies of the two islands have done remarkably well. Jersey's GDP, for instance, rose 90 percent in real terms between 1980 and 1990. Economic performance in the Channel Islands proves once again that the efficiency, simplicity, and fairness induced by a flat tax have a positive influence on economic growth, employment, and the overall standard of living.

In addition, their treasuries have gained too: In 1990, income tax receipts accounted for 74 percent of total government revenue in the case of Guernsey and an impressive 90 percent in the case of Jersey.[16]

HONG KONG: FLAT TAX PIONEER AND ECONOMIC MIRACLE

With the exception of the tiny Channel Island of Jersey, Hong Kong is the mother of all flat-tax regimes, having gone this route in 1947. Hong Kong's system is unusual, though. Tax policymakers everywhere could profit from a study of Hong Kong's dual tax system. It is fair to lower-income taxpayers and rewards hard work and economic success.

Here's how Hong Kong's dual system of salary taxation works. One system taxes the income of Hong Kong residents with four graduated tax brackets. Hong Kong's brackets, in contrast with ours, are extremely low and simple (you don't lose deductions when your income reaches certain thresholds as you do in the U.S.) ranging from 2 percent to a high of 20 percent.

The personal income tax allows for a limited number of deductions, most notably for charitable contributions—up to 25 percent of your net income (raised from 10 percent since the 2002-03 tax year) and for home-loan interest deductions. The system also includes single and married personal allowances, child allowances, other dependent-care deductions, and a pension deduction.

Alternatively, there's the flat-tax option. If a taxpayer's tax liability exceeds 16 percent of his income, then he can opt for the 16 percent flat tax. This 16 percent rate is referred to as the "standard rate."

Under the dual system, about 1 percent of Hong Kong taxpayers elect to pay the flat tax. According to the Inland Revenue Department, (the Hong Kong tax collection agency), 12,328 taxpayers paid taxes under the standard rate in the 2002-03 tax year period. Though this number is only 1 percent of all taxpayers, the money paid by this group accounted for more than 21 percent of Hong Kong's salary tax revenues.[17]

The fact that a flat tax is so simple that it can used in tandem with a traditional graduated-rate system highlights the flexibility of the flat tax.

But you think this is too complicated to work in the U.S.? Yet we too have a dual system under the present tax code: we have to pay either according to our own traditional income tax system or via the Alternative Minimum Tax. It's a dual system, but unlike Hong Kong's, it does-n't offer you a choice. And the liability you choose has to be the more painful one—which is why I'm only half joking when I say that the AMT should really be called the Alternative Maximum Tax.

The tax system of Hong Kong features some of the most transparent and fair components of any system in the world. In addition to its extremely low rates, Hong Kong does not double-tax dividends, as does the U.S. There are no capital gains taxes. And for those living and working in Hong Kong, a tax treaty with Mainland China (Hong Kong is labeled a special administrative region) eliminates the risk of simultaneous taxation by both governments.

Again, unlike the U.S., Hong Kong's rate of taxation on business profits is extremely low. Corporations pay 17.5 percent of profits to the tax collector, after normal deductions for expenses, including generous depreciation allowances. Small businesses do slightly better, paying only 16 percent on profits. The profits tax in Hong Kong accounts for about 32 percent of total tax revenues, compared with approximately 9 percent for most other Organization for Economic Co-operation and Development (OECD) countries.

Recent history has been no bed of roses for this small spec of the earth's real estate. Hong Kong is currently emerging from a difficult period that began with 1997's financial crisis in Asia. Hong Kong's property market, a critical part of its economy, underwent a severe deflation, with prices plummeting 50 percent or more. The economy stalled, and there were budget deficits. When Hong Kong was handed over to China by Britain in 1997, its economy faced some uncertainty over what would happen to its economic policy. This hurt domestic and overseas investment. And then Hong Kong was briefly devastated by the SARS scare of 2003.

Hong Kong, however, has moved past these obstacles and is once again experiencing economic growth.

Hong Kong's economic history supports its free-market foundations and the flax tax. In 1960, Hong Kong's per capita income was $3,249 (adjusted for inflation).[18] By 2003, Hong Kong's per capita income was

$28,800, nine times higher than in 1960. And that figure is set to grow higher as its economy grows again.

Hong Kong today is one of the most advanced economies in the world. With a population of less than 7 million and a land mass of 402 square miles, Hong Kong boasts the 15th-highest GDP per capita in the world and is the world's 10th-largest trading entity and the 11th-largest banking center. All of this economic activity is centered in a geographic area one-fourth the size of our tiny state of Rhode Island.

Hong Kong is criticized for being, allegedly, over-reliant on property-related tax revenue. In the late 1990s and the early part of the twenty-first century, as property values dropped and property tax receipts fell, Hong Kong's traditional budget surpluses turned into deficits.

As a result, Hong Kong's standard tax rate was raised 1 percentage point to increase revenues. Still, 16 percent remains the highest tax anyone will have to pay on their personal income. That is the beauty of the Hong Kong tax system. Even when plunging property values forced the government to shift the tax base toward the income tax, it only had to boost the rate 1 percentage point.

Still, some critics want to see Hong Kong raise income taxes even more. But Hong Kong shouldn't jettison a tax system that has enabled it to grow so mightily.

There's no question that Hong Kong would have suffered even more had it had a more traditional, higher-tax rate system that most other countries suffer under. The slump would have been deeper and the recovery even slower. The purpose of government is not to eliminate deficits via high taxes if those high levies hurt the economy. The purpose of government is not to serve itself but to serve the broader public, to make greater prosperity possible for all. When critics in Hong Kong clamor that the flat tax must change, my advice is blunt: "Don't do it."

Hong Kong, Slovakia, Russia, and others are only the beginning of the move towards advocating and instituting flat tax. Countries in old Europe are studying the idea. Opposition parties are gaining strength advocating a flat tax in countries such as Poland, the Czech Republic, and Finland.

The spread of the flat tax around the world demonstrates the fact that the flat tax can and does work. In Russia, a 13 percent flat tax on income has successfully doubled government revenues in four short years. In Slovakia, a once-laggard, backward economy is turning itself into the next Irish miracle. In the Baltics, three small countries are now Westernized and growing at a good pace after making the extremely difficult transition from communist economies to free- enterprise economies.

In Hong Kong, the flat tax is working quietly alongside a low-rate progressive system that has helped to make Hong Kong one of the richest entities in the world. All of these nations are using the flat tax—and profiting. Why can't we?

THE U.S. NEEDS THE FLAT TAX TO COMPETE GLOBALLY

The growth of the flat tax movement overseas is part of a larger international movement toward tax simplification—one that has important implications for the U.S. as a global competitor.

When pundits bemoan threats to America's competitiveness, they usually focus on cheaper labor costs or more favorable regulatory policies abroad that are luring jobs and investment. They rarely consider the central role played by our tax policies.

America's tax code is one of the greatest influences on our ability to create capital here at home and to attract foreign capital—and thereby succeed in the world economy. Our taxation policies must be made more competitive if we are to remain the world's free-market leader.

America's taxes on profits—the combined federal and state tax rates—are about 40 percent, just about the *worst* among developed nations today, with the possible exception of Japan.

A recent study released by KPMG, one of the Big Four accounting firms, found the U.S. has the second- highest corporate tax rate among the 69 countries surveyed in the study. At the same time, the average corporate tax rate in Europe has fallen, on average, about 7 percentage points since 1996.[19]

The trend in Europe towards lower taxes and tax simplification has received relatively scant attention here. However, it is enabling countries to gain ground on the U.S. in the global economic race.

Austria, for instance, recently enacted a huge cut in the corporate tax rate—from 34 percent to 25 percent—with the intention of attracting businesses from nearby regions. Since this reform, potential investors have increased 60 percent and inquiries from Germany have more than doubled.[20]

Infineon, the semiconductor spin-off of Siemens, relocated its automotive industrial operations from Munich, Germany, to southern Austria in an effort to reduce its tax burdens.

Far better known is the case of Ireland, which transformed itself into a textbook model of business-risk-friendly tax reform in the late 1980s.

In 2003, Ireland cut its basic corporate tax rate to the breathtakingly low level of 12.5 percent. Ironically, it made the move in response to complaints from EU partisans of tax "harmonization" who hoped that Ireland would even out its former system of taxation. At the time, its corporate rates varied from 10 percent to 30 percent. EU bureaucrats wanted Ireland to make its rate an across-the-board 30 percent—in effect, a tax increase. Instead the Irish boldly adopted a low 12.5 percent rate.

Ireland entered the European Union in the 1970s as one of the EU's poorest members. Ireland's per capita income today is about 7 percent higher than the per capita income of Britain, France, and Germany.

The nation has been steadily attracting high-tech companies—many of them from the U.S. chipmaker Intel, which has invested heavily in the Irish economy since the late 1980s. By the end of 2004, it had poured some $5 billion into Ireland. Its Leixlip plant, 45 minutes south of Dublin, has created some 4,200 jobs.[21] Internet auction giant eBay recently opened a new European office in Ireland that will employ 800 people. Google opened its new European headquarters in Dublin in 2004, creating 150 jobs. It expects to add about 100 more jobs in the not-too-distant future.[22]

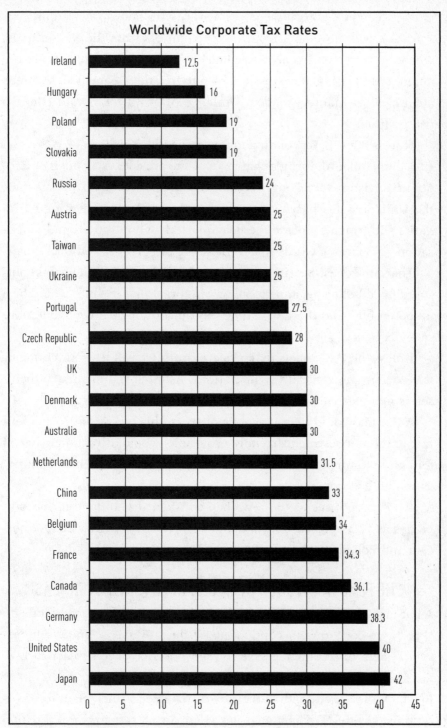

Worldwide Corporate Tax Rates

Country	Rate
Ireland	12.5
Hungary	16
Poland	19
Slovakia	19
Russia	24
Austria	25
Taiwan	25
Ukraine	25
Portugal	27.5
Czech Republic	28
UK	30
Denmark	30
Australia	30
Netherlands	31.5
China	33
Belgium	34
France	34.3
Canada	36.1
Germany	38.3
United States	40
Japan	42

McAfee, the California-based software firm known for its antivirus software, will move its European headquarters from the Netherlands, where corporate profits are taxed at 31.5 percent, nearly three times the amount McAfee will have to relinquish to Ireland. Meanwhile, McAfee's chief rival, Symantec, made a similar move to the Emerald Isle two years earlier.

How is the U.S. responding to this competitive challenge? We're not. R. Glenn Hubbard, former chairman of the president's Council of Economic Advisors, told Congress that, "From an income tax perspective, the United States has become one of the least attractive industrial nations in which to locate the headquarters of a multinational corporation."[23] Sobering words that underscore the urgent need for reform.

The same chest-beating pundits and politicos who rail against outsourcing, off-shoring, and globalization forget that the U.S. would be a lot better off—and there would be less outsourcing—if we had a more sane tax policy.

Unless the U.S. enacts major tax reforms, we will lose our competitive edge to more fiscally agile nations. As other nations make themselves more attractive to capital, our advantage will wither.

A flat tax would help us enormously in this task. That 17 percent rate and the investment-friendly provisions would attract a gusher of foreign investment while unleashing even more entrepreneurial innovation here at home.

If 17 percent seems too low, then consider that Ireland taxes companies at 12.5 percent, Lithuania at 15 percent, Hungary at 17.7 percent and Poland at 19 percent.

THE FLAT TAX WOULD HELP U.S. COMPANIES OVERSEAS

A flat tax would remove the unfair burden imposed by our tax code on U.S.-based corporations conducting business overseas. Under our current system of worldwide taxation, corporations are subject to U.S. taxes on income that they earn overseas. They pay taxes to the country in which they operate; then they are also liable to Uncle Sam for taxes on those profits. For instance, say Company X sets up shop in Hong

Kong and makes $20 million in taxable profit. The company would have to pay 17.5 percent of this profit in corporate taxes to the Hong Kong Inland Revenue Department. Then it would be required to shell out another 17.5 percent of its profits to the IRS to satisfy the 35 percent U.S. corporate tax if it brought those profits home. Yes, companies get a tax credit for taxes paid overseas. But the net effect is still a higher—and disadvantageous—tax burden on American-based companies.

It should come as no surprise that over $600 billion of overseas profits of American companies have been parked overseas—if the money had been brought to the U.S., it would have faced taxes. America was deprived of that capital and, thus, our economy lost out. In 2004, Congress granted a temporary tax holiday as an incentive for companies to repatriate that money back to the U.S.

Companies are responding. Johnson & Johnson, for example, is bringing back $11 billion; Schering-Plough, $9 billion; and Pfizer, up to $38 billion. Of course, the question this raises is: If we can cut the worldwide taxation rate *temporarily*, why can't we make it low *permanently*?[24]

In contrast, other nations employ a territorial system that taxes only the business that is conducted on their soil. To take our hypothetical Hong Kong example, if the U.S. had a territorial system, Company X would only pay Hong Kong a profits tax and would owe nothing to the IRS.

Companies headquartered in nations with this kind of territorial corporate tax system have a huge edge over U.S.-based businesses operating overseas, especially in countries like Ireland that have low corporate tax rates.

America's worldwide tax system is damaging our competitiveness. International tax rules covering multinational businesses account for 44 percent of the cost of compliance for our largest companies.[25] Doing away with our worldwide tax system would not only eliminate this huge burden of complexity, but would also help U.S. companies compete on a level playing field.

Some critics argue that companies that operate abroad cost America jobs here at home. Not really. Commerce Department data demonstrate that most of overseas companies' sales are to overseas customers. Only 11 percent of the sales of U.S.-owned foreign companies are to American consumers.[26]

American companies with foreign operations account for almost one-fourth of all U.S. exports. Do we wish to harm this export capability?

Adopting territorial taxation as part of a flat tax would help U.S. companies to retain their leadership position and their competitiveness.

The United States can learn from the success of other nations that have made tax reform a priority. We can learn, as we have seen, from our own past comebacks after economic adversity. We must not forget that thanks to Ronald Reagan's free-market, low-tax policies in the 1980s, the U.S.'s once-stagnant economy rebounded and achieved extraordinary success, even in the face of increased global competition. As the late *Wall Street Journal* editor Bob Bartley noted, America's growth in terms of its Gross Domestic Product exceeded the entire size of West Germany's economy.

Some fear that globalization will weaken America's ability to compete. Obviously parts of our economy are now going through a difficult time, especially manufacturing. But the American economy has been undergoing major changes for most of its existence.[27]

If we have the right incentives here at home, we will more than hold our own and, despite changes, continue to provide most Americans with a higher standard of living.

A flat tax is the best option to insure that America remains an attractive place for international investors to direct their money and for homegrown entrepreneurs to take risks to create new products and services. In short, a flat tax is a critical part of keeping America the chief innovator in the world.[28]

CHAPTER SEVEN

Why the Naysayers Are Flat Out Wrong

The evidence is there. The flat tax will work. It will provide a tax cut that will energize the country. It will free up the brainpower and capital to usher in an era of productivity and prosperity. It will improve our quality of life by lifting tax-related anxieties and hassles, freeing us from having to waste our energies on useless endeavors—from gathering volumes of records to making unnecessary investments for tax purposes. In doing this, it will increase our ability to choose how we want to live and work, create and spend our wealth.

The flat tax would make us a better society—just as it is doing in the many countries around the globe that are using it.

Yet that is not what the naysayers will tell you. They insist that the flat tax would harm charitable giving, home ownership, fiscal soundness in Washington, municipal bonds, health care, and much else. They cynically portray the flat tax as a "giveaway to the rich" and an "oppressor of the poor." They insist that the it will do everything except unleash the ten plagues.

Their criticisms have been widely reported. What has gone largely unrecognized are their self-interested motivations, like the those of the politicians who have criticized the flat tax because of unrelated personal agendas, or tax-preparation firms that launched campaigns against tax simplification because they fear it might put them out of business.

And so their perspectives are allowed to influence people who are afraid of change, whose first impulse when considering a new idea is to think "this won't work" instead of seeing why it can.

As this chapter demonstrates, the naysayers are flat out wrong about the flat tax. Their worries and criticisms are easily disposed of. In fact, as you will see, *the flat tax will*

- help boost charitable giving;
- expand homeownership as well as increase the value of existing homes;
- improve Washington's tax receipts;
- make health care more affordable;
- and bring more accountability to state and local governments.

The flat tax will do these things and more.

THE FLAT TAX WILL INCREASE CHARITABLE GIVING

One of the most damning criticisms made by opponents of a flat tax is that it would curtail charitable giving by eliminating the tax deduction for donations. This is simply not the case. *Charitable giving would actually be helped by a flat tax.*

Americans have always been a generous people. The response to the 9/11 attacks demonstrated this. Americans donated more than $2 billion after that terrible event. We saw a similar phenomenon after the devastating tsunami in southeast Asia.

As people across the nation reached for their checkbooks to help those devastated in New York and Washington and then in Asia, it's doubtful many were thinking about the tax code.

In fact, under our current system, only 31.5 percent of all taxpayers are eligible to deduct their charitable donations.[1] The rest simply take the standard deduction. In 2003 these non-itemizers accounted for nearly $39 billion in donations, or 20 percent of total individual giving.

Generous as we are with our money, Americans still give even more—our time. According to Independent Sector's *Giving and Volunteering in the United States, 2001* study, Americans volunteer at least 15.5 billion hours a year. The study placed a value of $239 billion on these volunteer hours.

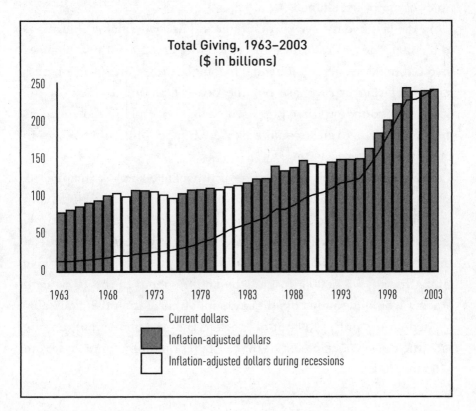

Total Giving, 1963–2003
($ in billions)

Fair enough, an opponent would argue. But the fact remains that the vast majority of individual giving is done by those taking advantage of the tax deduction. That's true. *But they don't choose the amount they give based on those breaks.*

All you need to do is look at historical information on charitable giving before and after major modifications to top income tax rates to see what impact these changes had on charitable giving.

The surprising answer? Hardly any.

Take a look at the chart on the previous page that shows total U.S. charitable giving over the forty-year period from 1963 to 2003.

Two things should stand out. First, as our economy has grown over the last three decades, so has charitable giving. It's pretty simple: When people have more to give, they give more. Second, charitable giving has generally declined or remained flat during periods of economic recession. But there are no spikes—upward or downward—in response to times of major tax changes.

In the last twenty-five years, Congress has made major alterations to the tax code several times. In 1981, 1986, and 2003, those changes involved notable cuts in individual income tax rates. In 2001 Congress passed legislation to phase out the death tax. During most of the debates surrounding these proposed changes, people raised concerns that lowering tax rates would adversely impact philanthropy. Yet in each case, they were wrong.

President Reagan's 1981 tax reform package slashed income tax rates across the board and dropped the highest levy from 70 percent to 50 percent. If the critics had been right, this cut would have sharply reduced charitable giving, since Americans would be able to deduct a smaller percentage of their donations and presumably would give less. After all, a $1,000 gift made by an individual in the 70 percent bracket would actually cost that person, after he took the charitable tax deduction, only $300 out-of- pocket. But at a 50 percent tax rate rate, the out-of-pocket cost of that $1,000 donation would rise from $300 to $500.

But the drop-off in philanthropy never happened. Charitable giving in 1984, the year when the tax cut was fully in effect, was 11.8 percent higher than it had been in 1980. Total giving rose from 1.7 percent of GDP in 1980 to 1.8 percent for 1984.[2]

As Stuart Butler at the Heritage Foundation has pointed out, "Between 1980 and 1984, the amounts contributed by donors in every category (individuals, corporations, foundations, and bequests) increased, as did the levels of contributions received by nonprofits in every category (from the arts to human-services organizations). And these increases occurred despite the 1981–82 recession."

Similar concerns were expressed about the 1986 tax reform (an action that politicians have since spent most of the time undoing). This bill lowered the top individual tax rate from 50 percent to 28 percent and eliminated the rule that allowed all taxpayers—whether they itemized or not—to deduct charitable contributions from taxable income between 1981 and 1986.

Professional worrywarts—who learned nothing from the success of the 1981 measure—again predicted that the sky would fall on philanthropic contributions. A report by Independent Sector, a coalition of non-profit and philanthropic interests, even predicted that charitable giving would decline by $8 billion because of the 1986 tax bill.

Once again, these critics were misguided. As Butler describes it:

Total donations did fall by 1.3 percent between 1986 and 1987 (by $1.01 billion in current dollars), but the 1986 total had been a sharp 16.1 percent higher than the total in 1985. This 1986 "blip" was most likely due to donors' having advanced giving originally planned for 1987 to 1986 to take account of that year's larger tax break. Donations then rose strongly again in 1988 and 1989, even though the final rate reductions of the 1986 act were being phased in. Taken together, contributions in inflation adjusted dollars rose by 19.1 percent between 1985 and 1989, slightly above the historical increase for similar periods. Far from the bleak outcome predicted by analysts, charitable contributions actually

increased after enactment of the 1986 tax bill—again, principally as a
result of strong economic growth.[3]

The bottom line is remarkably simple: As the economy goes, so goes
charitable giving. Generally speaking, giving to charity represents a
certain percentage of national income, usually around 2 percent.
Over the past 40 years, charitable giving as a whole has amounted to
no less than 1.7 percent of GDP and no more than 2.3 percent of
GDP. It doesn't take a Ph.D. in economics to guess what the best way
to boost giving is. When our economy expands, giving expands.
Therefore, boosting our economy would boost the flow of donations
to charity.

We can look to the stock market for another illustration of how giving parallels economic performance. According to Patrick Rooney,
Director of Research at the Center on Philanthropy, "[the] strongest
predictor of individual giving is the S&P 500. If other factors are held

Some argue that abolishing the death tax will create British-Euro-
pean like aristocracies that would dominate and manipulate our country. Actually, abolition of the death tax would do just the opposite—it
would speed up the breakup of great family fortunes. Think about it.
Today's death tax compels tax pros to devise elaborate trusts and
schemes to preserve major family fortunes. If there were no death tax,
the assets would more likely be passed on directly to younger generations. Human nature being what it is, a good number of these folks
will rapidly spend chunks of that money. Ensuing generations are not
as likely to be as frugal, hardworking or as entrepreneurially innovative as the individual or generation that initially created the wealth.
And if they were, we would benefit from their innovations and wise
investments. With the absence of a death tax, it is likely that there
would be more direct bequests, which would recycle fortunes into the
rest of the economy's population more quickly.

constant, a 100 point increase in the index is associated with a $1.7 billion increase in charitable giving."[4] If we really want to see our national giving go through the roof, we should do everything we can to make our economy grow.

We have further proof that tax incentives are not what cause people to donate. A 1996 poll found that among people who make charitable donations, "keeping taxes down" came in at the bottom of a list of several reasons for donating to charity.

The groundlessness of fears about the impact of tax relief on charitable giving is illustrated by the controversy over the death tax (see box). Liberals love to berate the wealthy and then abscond with their wealth when they die. Many analysts complain that by abolishing the death tax, we would do away with any incentive the rich may have to donate their fortunes to charity.

Indeed, current law allows for unlimited deductions for charitable contributions. These analysts claim, as they do for the tax deduction for living donors, that the death tax lowers the "price" of giving because to donate money is to avoid taxation. This wrongheaded thinking first of all assumes that the wealthy would never give to charity without being forced to and then assumes that the government knows better how to manage someone's hard-earned savings and assets accumulated over a lifetime.

Just look at what happened when President Bush's plan to phase out the death tax passed in 2001. Some analysts were concerned that bequests from estates would drop. But in 2003 bequests actually rose 10.3 percent in real dollars to $21.6 billion.[5] Recall that in both 2001 and 2003, there were reductions in personal income tax rates which, theoretically, should have hurt giving. That didn't happen.

Dying should not be a taxable event. A flat tax will free up money for charitable donations that would have been taxed away by an insidious tax that will be killed off, once and for all, under my plan.

Studies show that tax law changes do little to affect the level of giving. Only the timing of giving is affected. In other words, a system that repeals the death tax will see donors giving away more money while they are alive, eliminating the need for complicated trusts and death-tax avoidance measures.

The best way to increase gifts to nonprofits is to promote economic growth through sound fiscal policy—especially enacting a flat tax. Why should the government be allowed to swoop down like a vulture and ravage your estate, and the wealth you leave your family, after you die?

"THE FLAT TAX WILL DRAIN THE TREASURY"—WRONG!

Critics of a flat tax worry that it won't generate enough revenue for Uncle Sam. In their simplistic minds, lower rates automatically mean lower receipts for the government. But most estimates of tax receipts are based on assumptions about taxpayer behavior and economic growth that bear little relation to reality.

As we've mentioned in chapter four, the Congressional Budget Office, the Office of Management & Budget, and the Treasury Department all predict the outcome of tax code changes based on a technique known as "static analysis." It's founded on the belief that our behavior will remain static in response to either tax increases or reductions. It's a wrongheaded assumption, and an especially ironic one when you consider how much time Congress spends on social engineering, trying to change our behavior through those very tax increases or cuts that the analysts says we're not supposed to respond to!

Static analysis has two major flaws. It doesn't sufficiently account for what happens to the economy after a tax cut: the boost in activity that occurs when dollars that would have been spent on taxes are funneled into productive investments such as additional machinery, renovations or hiring new employees. All of this adds to the economy and expands the tax base.

When estimates of the effects of tax code changes are made using static analysis, cutting taxes is always portrayed, wrongly, as resulting in a permanent loss in Uncle Sam's tax receipts.

A second and far bigger flaw of static analysis is that it ignores how lower tax rates act as an incentive to productive behavior. Think of it this way: If people's incomes were taxed at a 100 percent rate on Mondays and a zero percent rate on Tuesdays, how many people do you think would show up for work on Monday?

The answer, of course, is none. Who would show up for work on a day when all their money would be taxed away? They'd show up the following no-tax day. And yet Washington's static analysts, mired in their rigid, wrongheaded theories, would have you believe the opposite. They'd swear up and down that attendance would be the same on Mondays as it would be on Tuesdays.

When attempting to assess the likely impact of proposed tax policies, the government's use of static analysis has translated into consistent cluelessness—generating misinformation that is all too often accepted, without question, by the media and general public. Some examples:

- In 1989, Bob Packwood (R-OR) requested a revenue forecast from Congress's Joint Committee on Taxation (JCT) on a hypothetical tax increase raising the top rate to 100 percent on incomes over $200,000. The JCT responded by forecasting increased revenues of $204 billion in 1990 and $299 billion in 1993.[6] *Essentially, the JCT predicted that people would continue to work even if the government taxed them out of every penny they earned.*
- The Congressional Budget Office predicted that the 1986 corporate tax rate increase would raise government revenues from $89 billion to $101 billion. In reality, corporations altered business practices and revenues decreased to $84 billion.[7]

And these are only two examples. *The truth is that our federal government has consistently and grossly underestimated tax collections that result from tax cuts and overvalued the so-called windfalls in revenue expected from tax increases.*

The 1986 capital gains tax hike from 20 percent to 28 percent did *not* result in higher revenues. Instead, realized gains jumped from $172 billion to $328 billion the year *before* the increase and fell dramatically in the years following it, to $112 billion in 1991.[8]

In 1978 the Steiger Amendment (named after the late Bill Steiger, a Congressman from Wisconsin who had acutely understood the devastating effects the then- catastrophic capital gains tax rate had on innovation), slashed the maximum capital gains levy from nearly 50 percent to 28 percent. The tunnel-visioned estimators predicted revenues would plummet.

Instead capital gains realizations went from $51 billion in 1978 to $73 billion in 1979. Federal tax receipts went from $9.3 billion to $11.7 billion and increased each successive year.[9]

Again, in 1997, the government failed to correctly estimate the actual revenue that would roll in when the capital gains tax was reduced from 28 percent to 20 percent (recall that it had been raised in 1986). The government assumed that realized capital gains would be unchanged by the cut and forecast that total realized capital gains in 1997 would be $205 billion. Their estimates were completely wrong. Actual capital gains were $365 billion, 78 percent higher than predicted. Capital gains tax revenue was 44 percent higher *despite* the 29 percent reduction in the rate at which gains were taxed!

The government's estimates missed the mark by ever-wider margins in the next two years so that by 1999 the original capital gains estimate was off by $325 billion. Capital gains tax revenues were 50 percent higher than forecast.[10]

Government analysts made these spectacularly wrongheaded forecasts because their static analysis totally ignores the consequences of lower taxes: the upsurge of activity by entrepreneurs investing, innovating, and developing tomorrow's iPods or life-lengthening, life-improving medicines. They fail to see that the resulting larger, richer economy would generate more revenue. Consequently, Uncle Sam will collect more incomes taxes, profits taxes, payroll taxes, and numerous other exactions that would more than make up for the absence of capital gains tax receipts.

As these examples show, static analysis has failed so often that one wonders whether it should be accepted as analysis at all. An alternative now gaining favor is often called either dynamic analysis or dynamic scoring. Dynamic analysis estimates the positive effect of

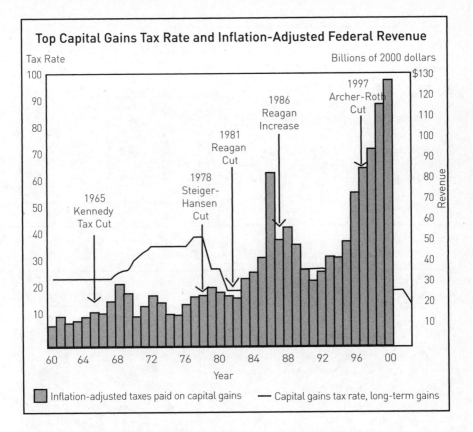

Top Capital Gains Tax Rate and Inflation-Adjusted Federal Revenue

Tax Rate   Billions of 2000 dollars

1997
Archer-Roth Cut

1986
Reagan
Increase

1981
Reagan
Cut

1978
Steiger-
Hansen
Cut

1965
Kennedy
Tax Cut

Year

■ Inflation-adjusted taxes paid on capital gains   — Capital gains tax rate, long-term gains

1997 Capital Gains Tax Rate Cut: Actual Revenues vs. Government Forecast (in $billions)

	1996	1997	1998	1999	2000
Long-Term Capital Gains Tax Rate	28%	20%	20%	20%	20%
Net Capital Gains:					
Pre-Tax Cut Estimate (January 1997)	--	$205	$215	$228	N/A
Actual	$261	$365	$455	$553	$644
Capital Gains Tax Revenue:					
Pre-Tax Cut Estimate (January 1997)	--	$55	$65	$75	N/A
Actual	$66	$79	$89	$112	$127

Source: Congressional Budget Office, and U.S. Department of the Treasury, Office of Tax Analysis.

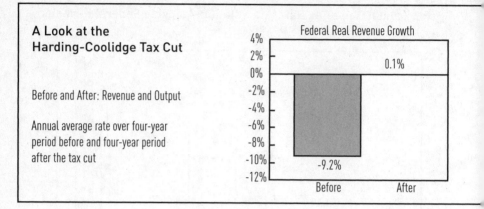

A Look at the Harding-Coolidge Tax Cut

Before and After: Revenue and Output

Annual average rate over four-year period before and four-year period after the tax cut

Federal Real Revenue Growth

- Before: -9.2%
- After: 0.1%

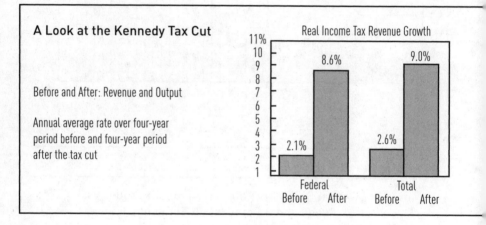

A Look at the Kennedy Tax Cut

Before and After: Revenue and Output

Annual average rate over four-year period before and four-year period after the tax cut

Real Income Tax Revenue Growth

- Federal Before: 2.1%
- Federal After: 8.6%
- Total Before: 2.6%
- Total After: 9.0%

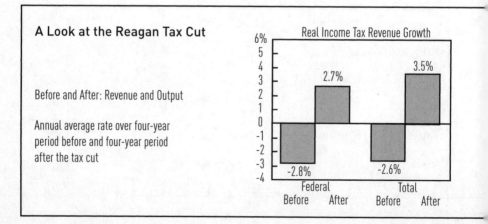

A Look at the Reagan Tax Cut

Before and After: Revenue and Output

Annual average rate over four-year period before and four-year period after the tax cut

Real Income Tax Revenue Growth

- Federal Before: -2.8%
- Federal After: 2.7%
- Total Before: -2.6%
- Total After: 3.5%

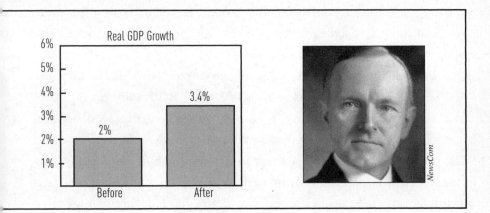

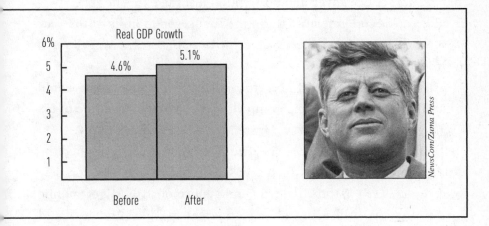

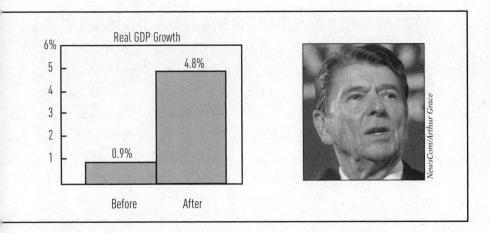

cutting taxes and accounts for the growth in the economy that is a result of the increased incentives for more productive work and additional risk-taking.

However to date the method has been implemented half-heartedly and acceptance has been slow. In 2003 the CBO finally produced a study using dynamic scoring. It was an analysis of President Bush's budget proposal, projecting the impact of that budget on the economy. The project, alas, was only a small first step, and a disappointing one at that. The CBO *still* underestimated the upward tick the economy gets when tax rates are cut. In the real world, the good of the Bush tax cuts *overwhelmed* any damage done by higher government spending. His cuts did *not* reduce government revenues; just the opposite. They triggered greater economic growth. In the first seven months of the year 2005, Washington's tax collections are up over 10 percent over those of the prior year.

Estimating the effects of tax reform using dynamic analysis would result in a more accurate and compelling picture of the volume of tax revenue that would be generated by reforms such as the flat tax.

If our government forecasters effectively and correctly applied the tools of dynamic analysis, which is based on real world behavior, they would quickly see that the flat tax would enormously boost economic growth and the well-being of the American people. And it would improve the finances of our government.

THE FLAT TRUTH ABOUT THOSE MORTGAGE DEDUCTIONS

"But I'd lose my mortgage deduction." That's a frequent objection voiced by critics of the flat tax. It's true. You would lose the mortgage interest deduction under the flat tax. But to those people who fear this our answer is: Think of it as the price of liberation. The loss of this deduction will be more than offset by what you gain under a flat tax system.

But just don't take my word for it. Let's go back and look at the facts. The current tax code allows homeowners to shield income from taxation equal to the interest they pay on certain mortgages. (Under the

1986 Tax Act, the mortgage interest deduction can only be taken on mortgage interest on loans up to a value of $1 million.)

And so millions of American homeowners each year deduct the interest payments on their home mortgages from their taxable income to lower their tax bill.

This deduction can be substantial. For example, an individual earning $60,000 who has a $200,000 mortgage on a $250,000 home can end up with a total deduction—on mortgage interest and on property taxes on the home (which also would not be deductible under the flat tax)—of, say, $18,000 under our current code. That means he'd pay taxes on $42,000 instead of $60,000 in income. No wonder why people in high tax states such as New York and California are especially afraid of losing this tax break.

Flat tax opponents argue that many Americans depend on the mortgage deduction to buy a home. But in fact, only 28.6 percent of those who filed income tax returns claimed the mortgage interest deduction.[11] And, as you would expect, the deduction favors those with higher incomes. Taxpayers at the higher tax brackets reap a tax break in proportion to their tax rate. Low-income earners in the 15 percent bracket, for instance, only get 15 cents back for every dollar of interest they claim. Those in the highest tax bracket of 35 percent get back 35 cents on the dollar.

This results in a disproportional benefit for taxpayers earning more than $100,000. They claim almost 36 percent of all the mortgage deductions in a given year, even though they represent only 8 percent of tax filers. On the other hand, those with earnings less than $50,000 claim only 24 percent of all mortgage interest deductions but account for 71 percent of taxpayers.[12]

It is therefore a misrepresentation to argue that eliminating the mortgage deduction would penalize low-income homeowners. Only 13 percent of taxpayers with adjusted gross incomes under $50,000 claim the mortgage tax deduction, and as we saw, taxpayers in lower brackets derive less benefit from this write-off because of the lower return on each dollar deducted.

Even so, opponents claim getting rid of the deduction will still take money out of homeowners' pockets. And, they add, hurting higher-income Americans will disproportionately hurt housing. These assertions are wrong. The flat tax would leave *more* money in homeowners' pockets, regardless of their income level.

The flat tax would be a boon for housing because not only would people keep more of their incomes but their assets would be higher. Remember what happened to housing prices when the capital gains tax on house sales was eliminated for most homeowners in the late 1990s? Housing prices zoomed upward.

The flat tax would get rid of the capital gains levy altogether. Not only would housing values soar—but also the value of other assets you own, particularly equities.

Here's something else opponents won't tell you: The flat tax would lower interest rates by about 20 percent. Robert Hall and Alvin Rabushka, economists and flat tax architects who did their ground-breaking work at Stanford University's Hoover Institution,[13] have pointed this out. Under the flat tax, lenders would no longer have to pay taxes on the interest revenue they receive from borrowers. As a result they can pass this saving along to their customers and interest rates would fall. This is not a theoretical assertion. Municipal bonds are free from double-taxation and thus have lower interest rates. A flat tax extends "muni" treatment to all debt instruments.

While borrowers would no longer be able to deduct their interest costs, they would instead get lower rates. It's simple, really. Our current treatment of lending is inefficient: We tax one party and give tax breaks to the other. A flat tax would remove the tax component and lower costs for everybody.

Other experts confirm the Hall-Rabushka thesis. Thus, if your mortgage is 6 percent today, you could refinance it at 5 percent or less if a flat tax were fully enacted.

The lower costs of lending would push interest rates down and, in effect, make borrowing for a home a less expensive proposition. The reduction in interest rates alone for home buyers would offset the elimination of the mortgage interest deduction. Additionally, as chapter 3 illustrates, a flat tax encourages investment and savings by eliminating the individual tax on capital gains, dividends, and interest. This increase in the pool of capital—assuming the Federal Reserve gives us a stable monetary policy—would also drive down interest rates.

The tax cut that would come with a flat tax would not only more than cover the loss of the mortgage interest deduction but also the loss of any deductions for property taxes. In other words, you'd still come out ahead—the taxes saved would be greater than the deductions you get from mortgages and property taxes under the current system.

So there you have it: A flat tax would mean higher income for you and lower interest rates on mortgages (and on everything else, of course). Bigger paychecks. Lower monthly mortgage payments. How in the world could this hurt housing?

But wait! What about those who purchased houses under the old system? Won't they feel that the rules have changed mid-stream and get hurt? No. Remember that taxpayers will have a choice between staying with the old convoluted and complex system or migrating to the flat tax. Given time, those who still battle the old tax code will acknowledge the benefits of the flat tax and choose to be subject to its simple and efficient rules.

Since a flat tax is a tax cut, you would end up with more money to spend, including for bigger homes.

"WON'T I LOSE DEDUCTIONS FOR STATE AND LOCAL TAXES?"

Critics whine that the flat tax would harm taxpayers by doing away with the deductions for state and local income taxes (and in some cases, sales taxes). Again, the flat tax is designed so that even without deductions, taxpayers still end up with a tax cut.

Anyway, why should Uncle Sam subsidize states that hit their citizens with high taxes? As a matter of fact, the loss of this deduction would be a boon for these beleaguered taxpayers—states would feel pressure to cut their exorbitant exactions. The experience of 1986 is instructive. Recall that this legislation got rid of many tax shelters and reduced the number of tax brackets and—key for our point here— whacked the top rate to 28 percent. High tax states howled: Suddenly the impact of their own high rates stung even more. In New York state, one dollar sent to Albany was, in effect, paid in half or 50 percent by Uncle Sam. Now it would be only 28 cents instead of 50 cents. Result: A number of states reduced their rates, including New York. We would see the same phenomenon again.

"WOULDN'T THE FLAT TAX KILL MY BENEFITS?"

We saw in chapter three how the current code helped create the problem of out-of-control healthcare costs. That raises the question: If healthcare were not deductible wouldn't businesses stop paying for it?

Indeed, some flat tax opponents are afraid of this. Actually, a flat tax, along with the creation of Health Savings Accounts by Congress in 2003, would make health insurance, and healthcare itself, more affordable, reversing today's trend towards ever-rising healthcare premiums that are placing healthcare insurance out of reach for millions of Americans.

By lowering the corporate tax rate from 35 percent to 17 percent, the loss of deductibility to businesses would be minimal. To retain valued employees, many companies would still offer fringe benefits or raise workers' pay. If you remember from chapter three, the need to retain valued people was why they began the practice, back in the 1940s, of paying for their health insurance in the first place.

Furthermore, a flat tax would be compatible with –and would not eliminate—new Health Savings Accounts, which were enacted in 2003. Health Savings Accounts, which let employees put away tax-free money to pay for health care, will become more prevalent in the coming years. They will be the salvation of the American health care system, because they will put consumers in charge of a growing portion of health care dollars. [See Appendix C]

A flat tax would eliminate economic distortions that have inflated the cost of health care and the cost of premiums. It would encourage a more accessible system that allows workers to see the money that goes into their health care. *Employees* will choose where to spend their money.

The flat tax is also good news for retirement benefits. It would remove contribution limits on retirement plans such as Roth IRAs and 401(k)s. In fact, the need for such vehicles would virtually disappear as all savings would be free of tax. On the corporate pension side, we would see a major expansion of the Roth IRA concept.

In effect, today's Roth IRA is basically a flat tax pension system. This type of IRA allows you to set aside after-tax money for retirement that can grow tax-free and be withdrawn tax-free anytime after you reach the age of 59 1/2. Taxes are paid only once—no double taxation. Currently a married couple, filing jointly, must earn less than $150,000 and an individual under $95,000 in order to be eligible for a Roth IRA. There is also currently a cap on Roth IRA contributions of $4,000 per year. ($4,500 if you are 50 or older). Again, a flat tax would permit unlimited contributions.

You wouldn't have to worry about limits on contributions or penalties on early withdrawals. No capital gains, no additional income taxes. You could decide how much to save each year, when to take it out and how to use it. The freedom and growth potential offered by a flat tax is unrivaled by the IRAs available under our current tax system.

An important factor to keep in mind is that today many company pension plans are in jeopardy—look at those in the airline industry or what happened to the pensions in many traditional steel companies. Federal pension insurance (the agency providing this insurance is losing money and may need a government bailout) does not guarantee that a retired worker will get all that his original pension plan promised. In many cases, workers' monthly pension payments suffered significant reductions when those plans were shifted over to the government after the companies that had initially provided their plans went bankrupt.

The nice thing about a Roth IRA-type of pension plan is that *you*, not the company, own it. It can't be taken away from you if your employer goes under.

A flat tax would help make defined contribution plans like the Roth IRA a larger part of our retirement savings—enabling them to replace the traditional pension system which is increasingly faltering.

"FLAT RATE HURTS THE POOR"—JUST THE OPPOSITE.

The worries of these flat tax critics could not be more off base. The flat tax would not hurt the poor—it would help them.

More than 58 million Americans have no income tax bills each year. However, all of these people still have to go through the hassle of filing a tax return or paying someone to fill it out for them. We have seen that low income people pay a higher percentage of their income to preparers than higher earning people do—4.5 percent. Those are dollars they can ill afford.

The simpler flat tax process would let them save this money. And many families would not have to pay taxes at all under the plan. Remember a family of four making up to $46,165 a year would pay no federal income taxes under the flat tax. And 42 percent of all returns—some 65 million—or—would be *non-taxable* by the year 2010.

Even if they do pay taxes, low income people will benefit from the plan's more generous exemptions—a $13,200 exemption for each adult in a family, compared with the $3,100 exemption in the current system. A married couple would receive exemptions totaling $26,400. If their income is less than that, they pay no taxes, even if one person is going to school and the other is making, say, $23,000 a year.

Child tax deductions are also generous. For every child or dependent, a family can claim a $4,000 deduction compared with $3,100 today. In addition, there is a $1,000 refundable tax credit for each dependent until they reach the age of 16—as is the case under a change made in the 2001 tax bill.

Low-income earners will get meaningful refunds without going through a tortuous process such as the current Earned Income Tax Credit, with its sliding scale and complicated formulas that usually require professional tax assistance to understand. (The EITC would still remain because it was put in place to, in effect, rebate Social Security payroll taxes for low-income workers. In the aftermath of a flat tax, the EITC would probably be changed, most likely as a part of a major overhaul of Social Security.) You would report your income on a one-page tax form. If you qualified, you'd get money back. It would be as simple as that.

The economic boom to be created by the flat tax would also help low income people by generating more jobs and higher wages. A great example is the boom of the 1980s, when President Reagan's tax cuts snapped this country out of the economic doldrums and led to rapid growth. Both GDP and employment expanded.

By accelerating economic growth, we will be providing opportunities to millions of Americans who might otherwise go jobless. And for those starting out or who currently lack the skills for higher-paying jobs, the flat tax would mean better after-tax pay in their current positions *and*, as the demand for labor rose, employers would have more incentive to train workers for better jobs. At the same time, we would be simplifying their tax lives, as well as providing refunds that would help poor working families make ends meet.

"FLAT TAX ONLY HELPS THE RICH"—NONSENSE

The flipside of liberal naysaying about the flat tax is that it would only help the rich. Wrong again. Liberal flat tax critics love to wave the tattered banner of class warfare to pit people of varying incomes against each other in the hope of derailing tax reform.

In fact, as we've seen, the flat tax is a tax cut for everyone. Not only that, it would *abolish* all those loopholes that are seen as benefiting the rich—the very tax breaks liberals love to hate. So why are they complaining?

The flat tax would in fact make it harder for those commanding armies of tax lawyers and lobbyists to manipulate the system. With the simplification brought about by the flat tax, everyone would be playing by the same rules. There would be no finagling by twisting and exploiting complicated rules and deductions.

Then there are the flat tax opponents who say the flat tax isn't fair because it doesn't tax the rich *enough*. Because they make more, they should pay more—and the government should get more from them.

This is sheer lunacy. The experiences of the 1960s and 1980s demonstrate that when tax rates are cut, the "rich" pay more. People in the top brackets have less incentive to shelter income—it becomes less cost-efficient. As we have seen, tax collections from high-income earners soared when their rates were cut. Before the Reagan tax cuts were passed in 1981, the top 1 percent of income earners paid 18 percent of federal personal income taxes. By 1988 they were paying more than 27 percent of the government's personal income taxes.

As for eliminating the death tax, perhaps the best, most persuasive overview was succinctly provided by Ramesh Ponnuru of the *National Review* (see Appendix B). The bottom line: You already paid taxes on your assets when you were alive. You should be able to leave this world unmolested by the IRS.

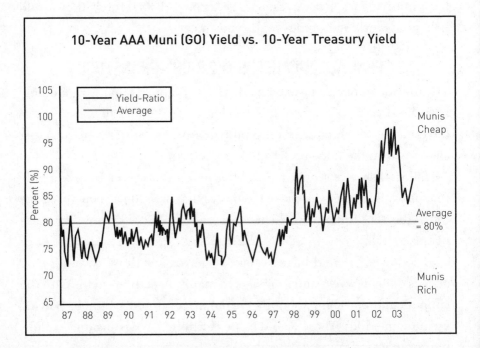

"WHAT HAPPENS TO TAX-FREE MUNICIPAL BONDS?"

Municipal bonds are exempt from federal taxes, and in many cases, state, or local taxes. Since their yields do not take a tax hit, they can offer lower interest rates in comparison with bonds that are not tax-free. Critics claim that, because the flat tax would make all bonds tax-free, investors would no longer have the incentive to put money into the lower-interest municipal bonds that are vital to the economic well-being of municipalities and states. Therefore, the naysayers grumble, states, cities and towns would be unable to build new schools, roads, or other infrastructure projects.

Again, this is nonsense. Many munis today offer yields that almost match the interest rates on taxable bonds. Historically, municipal interest rates have been about 80 percent of those of U.S. Treasury bonds. But at times, like now, this gap can shrink. Muni issuances have risen in recent years. Thus the ratio of muni to Treasury yields has increased to over 90 percent and sometimes even approaches 100 percent.

How would a flat tax affect your bond portfolio? It would, as we've said, essentially render all bonds tax-free. You'd be able to keep your interest payments. This would not affect the value of your existing tax-free bonds. But it would increase the value of your corporate and Treasury bonds. Their yields would decrease—and thus, their prices would go up.

In a total tax-free environment, people would still buy municipal bonds, but they'd pay more attention to credit quality and to what the money was actually being used for.

This would be good for government accountability. State and local governments and various government authorities may have to improve the quality of their projects to attract investors, since they'd no longer have the artificial tax advantages they currently enjoy. That would be a boon for taxpayers: Fewer white elephants, such as some of those sports stadiums you've been reading about recently; and more responsible fiscal policies.

"THE FLAT TAX WOULD HURT JOB CREATION"—ACTUALLY, IT WOULD CREATE JOBS

Then there are those critics who attack the flat tax based on the same convoluted argument they used to attack President Bush's 2003 tax plan.

That plan featured the temporary acceleration of the write-offs of capital investment. This, they feared, would cause employers to invest too heavily in capital spending. Companies would buy equipment and other items at the expense of hiring new people. These same people fear the flat tax would hurt job creation because it allows *all* business investment—not a part of it—to be immediately expensed.

Barry Ritholtz, chief market strategist of the Maxim Group and whose work was the impetus for much of the recent discussion, argues that, "If companies get a larger tax benefit for making bigger purchases, then jobs should be the natural result...but...labor requirements are much different in the age of intellectual property and software."[14]

According to his reasoning, innovations like management software and other technology allows companies to increase productivity without new hiring. "Thus," he concludes, "the unintended consequence of this twentieth-century solution [temporary accelerated depreciation] to a twenty-first century problem: Lackluster job growth."

Ritholtz acknowledges that this behavior is temporary, because the act itself creates only temporary incentives. As he wrote, purchases were "pulled through" from 2005 into 2004. Hiring is delayed and, therefore, "there is reason to hope that hiring will begin to swing upward in 2005."

What Ritholtz and others don't understand is that the flat tax would not create some temporary tax break for capital investment. Its low single tax rate creates an investment incentive which is *permanent*. Business owners would not be faced with fluctuating tax laws when deciding whether to use their financial resources to add employees or make capital purchases. Thus, no need to rush the purchase of a machine for fear a temporary tax credit might be lost. Neither capital nor labor would be given special treatment.

Under the flat tax, the 2003-2004 incentive that so concerned Ritholtz would be weak tea indeed. A flat tax would permit full, immediate write-offs of business capital spending. Buy a $100,000 piece of machinery and you'd have a $100,000 expense for tax purposes. Any losses could be carried forward to offset future profits.

The point bears repeating: Businesses would not be making their purchases early at the cost of hiring because there'd be no reason to hurry up and spend. The full expensing wouldn't have an expiration date. Today's law manipulates decision-making, and the unintended consequence is that this year's personnel budget became this year's capital investment budget.

In reality, a flat tax would hasten increases in our standard of living. There's often a long time lag between the creation of an innovation and its full development and use in the economy. The first successful transmission of television took place in 1927. But it wasn't until the 1950s that TVs become a common household item. Fax machines were first used in the late 1960s. Not until the 1980s did they become ubiquitous.

By encouraging more investment, a flat tax would *shorten* the time span between innovation and widespread use and dissemination. Our standard of living would be immeasurably higher as a result.

The flat tax would do anything but fulfill the fears of the naysayers. It would bolster our economy, encourage home ownership, and more affordable healthcare, increase government revenue and give the poor a real tax break—while eliminating the loopholes and complexity so often derided as abusive and unfair. A flat tax system would be the very opposite of what the naysayers tell you and would shrink today's tax beast down to size.

Isn't it an alternative worth trying?

CHAPTER EIGHT

How You Can Help Bring About Reform

So what can we do? How do we get out from under America's monstrous federal income tax code? How do we free ourselves from the grip of a nine-million-word beast that reaches into every corner of our lives, fills us with dread and loathing, saps our finances and creativity, and corrupts our way of life, as individuals and as a society?

Indeed, is it possible? Can we sweep away the countless regulations that have created the current morass? Can we undo the layers of damage, the complexity and confusion, that have built up over decades?

Not only that, can we overcome the naysayers and the doubters who are afraid of new ideas—and whose voices can sometimes drown out a full and reasoned consideration of the issues?

To those brave enough to ask, the answer is: We can do these things, and we *must*. Regardless of where we stand, most people agree that we cannot go on this way. America must reform its tax system. The future of our economy, of our nation—our quality of life, depends on it.

You do not have to take it anymore. There is an alternative: a fair and simple flat tax.

It is possible to institute a flat tax system. As we have seen, nations around the world with far fewer traditions of free enterprise have within the past few years taken the bold step of adopting a flat tax. And their economies have blossomed.

So what can we do? Reform movements are almost always an outgrowth of grass roots sentiment. Without a sustained public outcry, Washington will plug its ears and stick with the status-quo. This is where *you* come into the picture.

By joining the ranks of Americans who are fed up and ready for change, you can make a difference. Here are several steps you can take:

KNOWLEDGE IS POWER: KNOW THE ISSUES

Knowing what's happening on the tax front will give you the power to persuade others. Keep up on current tax issues and developments in the news. You don't have to be an expert to understand—and think critically—about general changes in the tax laws.

For example, Congress passed a corporate tax bill last October. If you read the *Wall Street Journal* or the *New York Times*, you'd know that the bill has more than $140 billion in tax breaks for all kinds of special interests—the latest layers of complexity to be added to the code.

Bone up on the news and issues using Internet search engines such as Google. And if possible, sign up for daily email news alerts that will send you links to stories on tax-related topics. Try keying in "flat tax." On December 12, 2004, such alerts would have yielded you four unique news stories about that subject.

If you use the Internet effectively, you'll sooner or later run across websites of the major advocacy groups. Organizations whose sites you can tap into include the National Taxpayers Union (on whose board I sit), Citizens Against Government Waste, The Tax Foundation, Americans for Tax Reform, and the and the Center for Freedom and Prosperity. These organizations, and other sources of information, should bring you up to speed.

In addition to these advocacy groups, there are think tanks that produce superb research such as the Heritage Foundation, the Cato Institute, the Institute for Research on the Economics of Taxation, the Tax Foundation, and many others.

Here is a list of tax policy-related organizations and websites you might find helpful as you explore the tax universe:

AMERICAN CONSERVATIVE UNION
http://www.conservative.org

AMERICANS FOR FAIR TAXATION
http://www.fairtax.org

AMERICANS FOR TAX REFORM
http://www.atr.org

ATLAS ECONOMIC RESEARCH FOUNDATION
http://www.atlasusa.org

BRADLEY FOUNDATION
http://www.bradleyfdn.org

CASCADE POLICY INSTITUTE
http://www.cascadepolicy.org/index.html

CATO INSTITUTE
http://www.cato.org

CENTER FOR THE DEFENSE OF THE FREE ENTERPRISE
http://www.cdfe.org

CITIZENS AGAINST GOVERNMENT WASTE
http://www.cagw.org

CITIZENS FOR A SOUND ECONOMY
http://www.cse.org

CLUB FOR GROWTH
http://www.clubforgrowth.org

DISCOVERY INSTITUTE
http://www.discovery.org

FAMILY RESEARCH COUNCIL
http://www.frc.org

FOUNDATION FOR ECONOMIC EDUCATION
http://www.fee.org

FOUND ON: THE FUTURE
OF FREEDOM FOUNDATION
http://www.fff.org/aboutUs/links.asp

FRASER INSTITUTE
http://www.fraserinstitute.ca

FREE ENTERPRISE FUND
http://www.freeenterprisefund.org

FREE MARKET MEDICINE
http://www.marketmed.org

FREE STATE PROJECT
http://www.freestateproject.org

HERITAGE FOUNDATION
http://www.heritage.org

HOOVER INSTITUTION
http://www-hoover.stanford.edu

HUDSON INSTITUTE
http://www.hudson.org

JOHN LOCKE FOUNDATION
http://www.johnlocke.org

LUDWIG VON MISES INSTITUTE
http://www.mises.org

MANHATTAN INSTITUTE
http://www.manhattan-institute.org

NATIONAL FEDERATION OF
INDEPENDENT BUSINESS
http://www.nfib.com

NATIONAL TAXPAYERS UNION
http://www.ntu.org

REPUBLICAN NATIONAL COMMITTEE
http://www.rnc.org

REPUBLICAN STUDY COMMITTEE
http://johnshadegg.house.gov/rsc

SCRAP THE CODE
http://www.scrapthecode.org

So now you know the key players. You're up on the news and the issues. Now you're ready to act.

THE NEXT STEP: CONTACT YOUR CONGRESSPERSON

Your local senator or representative is there to represent you. They're interested in the views of their constituents, the people who get them elected. Let them know that you support the flat tax.

If you're not sure who your congressperson is, you can find out by going to ***www.house.gov/writerep***, which has the name and contact information for each of our nation's representatives. The Senate has a similar site at ***www.senate.gov***.

Call your congressperson and your senators at their Washington, D.C., offices and ask to speak with their aide in charge of tax policy. Voice your support of fundamental tax reform and, specifically, a flat tax. When you call your representative or senator, make sure you mention that you are a constituent. Emphasize how important fundamental tax change is to you. Show that you're knowledgeable and energized about the flat tax cause.

Next step: Put it in writing. Write personal letters to your representative and senators stating why you believe the flat tax is the best option for simplifying the code and making the system fair and honest. This is where the research you've done should pay off.

Try to write in response to a specific news event. An informed letter is taken more seriously. For instance, you're writing in opposition to specific comments from a member of the Senate Finance Committee who said that tax reform would be difficult to accomplish. This actually happened in November. At the time, unfortunately, the senator's comments undermined reform efforts.

If only, back then, you had written, "I was disappointed to hear that you thought efforts at tax reform only amounted to 'tilting at windmills.' In the long run reforming our tax system is worth the political cost. I hope you will reconsider your support of tax reform so that I can support you in the next election."

A flood of such thoughtful opposition letters, with the help of some press coverage, would have demonstrated that opposition to the flat tax may not be as popular as the senator would have people believe.

We would have deprived the proponents of the status quo from having their customary last word—and for once let our side have its say.

Remember, your vote counts. And politicians know it. Let them know you will vote for candidates who support simplifying and lowering taxes.

Your letters shouldn't be too long. But if you're already politically active, you might squeeze in a sentence or two about who you are. You should get across that you have experience with educating voters, getting out the vote, volunteering on campaigns—in other words, you're an activist whose voice will continue to be heard on this issue.

Once you have written your senators and representative, don't stop there. Get your friends and relatives involved. Perhaps even some of your work colleagues might be interested. After all, every constituent who calls and writes is one more reason for our elected officials in Washington to support real reform.

WRITE ON: LAUNCH A ONE-MAN OR ONE-WOMAN LETTER WRITING CAMPAIGN

The next step is to write a letter to the editor of your local newspaper. If your community has more than one paper—such as a daily and a weekly—write them all.

When writing a newspaper, it's critical to write *in response to a news event*. The best time to write a letter to the editor is right after the newspaper runs a story on a tax topic, particularly if it discusses the flat tax or tax reform.

It really doesn't matter if the article you are responding to took a positive or a negative view of the flat tax or tax reform. In either case you have reason to write and express your views. You can praise the writer for getting it right or point out where the journalist went astray. Voice your opinions while reinforcing them with facts. Avail yourself of the ammunition within the pages of this book. Don't hesitate to use an example from your own experience.

When you agree with somebody in the newspaper, state your reasons for doing so. For instance, you might write, "Your editorial on tax cuts was right on the money. Cutting taxes is good for taxpayers and good for the economy. For example, when Reagan cut taxes in the 1980s . . ."

Again, it's important that you sound knowledgeable, trustworthy and not excessively emotional. Keep your letter short—to no more than three or four paragraphs. If you're writing a negative letter, keep a polite tone and avoid harsh or abusive language. Whatever you do, avoid profanity! You're writing that you disagree with the position of the article based on facts that the reporter or paper may have overlooked.

Try to make the tone of your letter similar to letters that the paper has previously published: You'll increase your chances of making the cut. If you've never written this kind of letter before, run it past someone else. Is it as clear and persuasive as you've intended? Get an honest outside opinion. Information about how to submit your letter is usually provided on the editorial page of your paper.

Once again, try to get friends to follow your lead by writing their own letters in support of the flat tax. But while they may take the same position, they should sound sufficiently different from yours. Editors aren't going to publish letters that are redundant.

START A BLOG

Starting a Web log to write about the flat tax and other tax issues would be a great way to put your tax knowledge to good use by building a community of people committed to tax reform. Blogs are one of the fastest-growing forms of communication today, particularly among the Internet savvy. Bloggers have been highly influential in a wide range of issues, to the chagrin of many in the old media. Dictionary publisher Merriam-Webster said that the word "blog" was the most popular word of the year in 2004, based on the number of people who logged onto Merriam-Webster's website looking for its definition.

Building a blog is easy. If you have an Internet connection and know how to type, you can have a blog. Setting one up takes only a few minutes. There are many sites that offer to host a blog for free. Some of the more popular sites are *www.blogger.com*, *www.blogspot.com*, or *www.livejournal.com*. Choose a site to host your blog. Follow the simple instructions to get started.

Once you've set up your site, you can start writing. Remember, consistent content is key. Frequently adding new posts to your flat tax blog will earn you loyal followers who will check back for more. The death of many blogs is that after the initial enthusiasm, they peter out. Never lose that sense of novelty. Regular postings and interesting commentary on the latest tax news will bring new visitors to your blog and keep old ones coming back. When you're established as a blogger, you may want to join a blog group. This is a collection of blogs published by people who share similar interests. By joining a tax issues blogging group, you would increase your exposure and hopefully glean insights from other people who are interested in changing the tax code.

DRAFT A PETITION AND COLLECT SIGNATURES

Another way to get involved is a good old-fashioned grass roots petition. Write a concise, compelling resolution demanding that your congressperson and U.S. senators support the flat tax. Then set a goal for—say, to collect 400–500 signatures—and then hit the pavement. Petitioning is a great opportunity to strike up conversations with people who many not have previously thought about the issue of tax reform. As you go, you'll get them thinking about the flat tax and how it would be the best solution to the mess we're in today. Check out **www.petitiononline.com** for free Web-hosting of petitions. You can write a petition and then post it online. Emailing or telling people to go sign it will help increase the number of petitioners.

An important tip: Choose one of your local representatives and target his or her constituents for your signature drive. That's the best way to get focus your representative's attention on your cause. Go after his voters.

If there has been a flurry of news about tax reform and you happen to be writing a letter to the editor—be sure to mention your petition efforts. That will only help get additional exposure for the cause.

CALL-IN TO TALK RADIO AND TELEVISION PROGRAMS

Numerous talk-radio and cable-TV shows permit call-ins from listeners and viewers. When the subject of taxes is in the news, don't hesitate to call-in and voice your support.

Some tips when calling in: Get to the point immediately. And, above all, be brief. Try to get your idea across in one or two sentences. You will have less than a minute—probably only a few seconds—to make your comment before the host moves on to the next caller. That's only enough time to comment on a single point. Don't ramble and veer off the topic. And above all, don't get emotional or personal—or for that matter, abusive. That's not to say you should be dull. Producers like lively, intelligent voices.

So now you know everything to know about flat tax reform. You've written your congressmen to call for tax simplification, you've spear-headed a letter writing campaign, a petition drive, started up a blog site, and you call in regularly to talk shows. Congratulations, you're now a flat-tax activist.

As you can see, the opportunities for promoting the flat tax are as endless as your imagination. Success in getting a flat tax hinges on the support of people like you. No amount of economic research and academic debate will lead to the passage of a flat tax. It's the outcry of citizens who just don't want to take it anymore. People like you who are fed up with the complicated, burdensome tax code, who are ready to slay the beast and bring about reform. We can't end the tyranny of the federal income tax code without activists like you contributing your voices to the cause. Are you ready? Our future and quality of life depends on you.

So what are you waiting for? Listed below are some additional resources you might find helpful in learning more about the flat tax and why it is right for America.

Resources

Flat tax books

- Dick Armey, *Flat Tax*. Ballantine, 1996.
- Daniel Mitchell, *The Flat Tax: Freedom, Fairness, Jobs and Growth*. Regnery, 1996.
- Douglas Sease and Tom Herman, *The Flat-Tax Primer: A Nonpartisan*

Guide to What It Means for the Economy, the Government—and you. Viking, 1996.

- Robert Hall, Alvin Rabushka, Dick Armey, Robert Eisner, Herbert Stein, *Fairness and Efficiency in the Flat Tax.* AEI Press, 1996.

- Robert Hall and Alvin Rabushka, *The Flat Tax.* Hoover Institute Press, 1995.

Other books

- Amity Shlaes, *The Greedy Hand: How Taxes Drive Americans Crazy and What to Do about It.* Random House, 1999.

- Milton Friedman, *Capitalism and Freedom.* University of Chicago Press, 2002.

Status of tax reform legislation

- S.1040—Tax simplification Act of 2003, sponsored by Sen. Richard Shelby

- H.R. 1040—Freedom Flat Tax Act, sponsored by Rep. Michael Burgess

- Look these bills up by number at *http://thomas.loc/gov/*

Members of the House of Representatives who support the flat tax:

- Rep. Roscoe G. Bartlett (MD)
- Rep. Rob Bishop (UT)
- Rep. John A. Boehner (OH)
- Rep. Henry Bonilla (TX)
- Rep. Michael Burgess (TX)
- Rep. Dan Burton (IN)
- Rep. Trent Franks (AZ)
- Rep. Ralph M. Hall (TX)
- Rep. Joel Hefley (CO)
- Rep. Jeb Hensarling (TX)
- Rep. Peter Hoekstra (MI)

- Rep. Jack Kingston (GA)
- Rep. Jeff Miller (FL)
- Rep. Sue Myrick (NC)
- Rep. Randy Neugebauer (TX)
- Rep. David Scott (GA)
- Rep. Pete Sessions(TX)
- Rep. Lamar Smith (TX)
- Rep. Cliff Stearns (FL)
- Rep. Lee Terry (NE)
- Rep. Dave Weldon (FL)
- Rep. Don Young (AK)

Senators who support the flat tax:

- Richard Shelby (AL)
- Larry Craig (ID)
- Arlen Specter (PA)

National Talk Radio Call-in numbers:

Al Franken Show
(Air America)
(866) 303-2270
thealfrankenshow@
airamericaradio.com

Alan Colmes Show
(Fox News Radio)
(212) 301-5800
alan@alan.com

Bev Smith Show
(American Urban
Radio Networks)
(412) 325-4197
Contact@thebevsmithshow.com

Bob Grant Show
(WOR)
(800) 321-8828
bobgrant@wor710.com

Clark Howard Show
(Cox Radio/Jones
Radio Networks)
(877) 87-CLARK
via clarkhoward.com

Coast to Coast w/George Noory
(Premier Radio Networks)
(800) 618-8255
george@coasttocoastam.com

Dave Ramsey Show
(The Dave Ramsey Show)
(888) TALK-BAK
daveonair@daveramsey.com

Doug Stephan Show
(Stephan Productions)
(888) 525-DOUG
doug@dougstephan.com

Dr. Laura Schlessinger Show
(Take on the Day, Inc.)
(800) DRLAURA
n/a

Ed Schultz Show
(Jones Radio Networks)
(877) 934-6833
edwardschultz@
clearchannel.com

G. Gordon Liddy (Radio America)
(800) GGLIDDY
liddyshow2@aol.com

Gene Burns Program (KGO)
(415) 808-0810
geneburns2@yahoo.com

Howard Stern Show
(c/o Don Buchwald & Assoc.)
(212) 867-1070
sternshow@howardstern.com

Howie Carr Show (WRKO)
(617) 266-6868
howiecarr@wrko.com

Imus in the Morning
(Westwood One)
(800) 370-4687
imus@msnbc.com

Janet Parshall Show (KGO)
(800) 343-9282
janet@jpamerica.com

Jerry Doyle Show (Talk Radio)
(800) 876-4123
askjerry@jerrydoyle.com

Jim Bohannon Show
(Westwood One)
(202) 457-7978
n/a

Jim Rome Show
(Premier Radio Networks)
(800) 636-8686
jimrome@netzero.com

John and Jeff Show (KLSX)
(323) 520-9710
johnandjeffshow@aol.com

Lars Larson Show
(KXL/Westwood One)
(503) 417-9595
lars@larslarson.com

Laura Ingraham Show
(Talk Radio)
(800) 876-4123
via lauraingraham.com

Mancow Muller Show
(WKQX/TRN)
n/a
mancow@mancow.com

Marc Bernier Show
(WNDB/WNDA/WFHG)
(800) 927-0033
marc@marcberniershow.com

Michael Medved Show
(Salem Radio)
(206) 621-1793
via michaelmedved.com

Michael Reagan Show
(Radio America)
n/a
mreagantalks@netscape.net

Michael Savage Show
(Talk Radio Network)
(800) 449-8255
michaelsavage@
paulreveresociety.com

Mike Gallagher Show
(Salem Radio)
(800) 655-MIKE
mike@mikeonline.com

MoneyTalk w/ Bob Brinker
(ABC Radio)
(800) 934-2221
bbmny2@aol.com

Morning in America w/
Bill Bennett
(Salem Radio)
(866) 680-6464
nburns@bennettmornings.com

Neal Boortz Show
(Cox Radio/Jones Radio)
(877) 310-2100
nealznuze@cox.com

News Beat w/ Blanquita Cullum
(Radio America)
(292) 408-0944
bq@radioamerica.org

O'Reilly Factor w/Bill O'Reilly
(Westwood One)
(212) 641-2000
oreilly@foxnews.com

Phil Hendrie Show
(Premier Radio Networks)
(866) 987-2570
phs@philhendrieshow.com

Randi Rhodes Show
(Air America)
(866) 303-2270
rrhodes@airamericaradio.com

Real Money w/ Jim Cramer
(WOR)
(800) 862-8686
jimcramer@wor710.com

Roger Hedgecock (KOGO)
(858) 569-TALK
roger@rogerhedgecock.com

Rollye James Show
(Mediatrix Syndicate)
(610) 640-6400
rollye@rollye.net

Rush Limbaugh Show
(Premier Radio Networks)
(800) 282-2882
rush@eibnet.com

Rusty Humphries Show
(Talk Radio)
(800) 449-TALK
via talk2rusty.com

Scott Hennen's Hot Talk
(WDAY)
(800) 279-WDAY
scott@wday.com

Sean Hannity Show
(ABC Radio)
(800) 941-7326
bill@kfi640.com

Small Business Advocate
w/ Jim Blasingame
(TSB)
(877) 287-4964
jim@jbsba.com

Stephanie Miller
(Jones Radio Networks)
(800) 783-7412
stephanie@stephaniemiller.com

The Money Pit w/
Fraeutler & Segrete
(888) MONEY PIT
tom@888moneypit.com

Thom Hartmann
(Thom Hartmann Program)
(866) 889-8894
thom@thomhartmann.com

Tony Snow Show
(Fox News Radio)
(866) 408-SNOW
tonysnow@foxnews.com

Arizona

"Nearly Famous"
Barry Young Show (KFYI)
(602) 258-KFYI
barryyoung@kfyi.com

Arkansas

Dave Elswick Show (KARN)
(800) 264-0092
Dave@karnnewsradio.com

California

Armstrong & Getty Show
(KSTE/KNEW)
(866) 331-TALK
armgetty@aol.com

Bill Handel Show (KFI)
(800) 520-1KFI
bill@kfi640.com

Glenn Beck Show
(Premier Radio Networks)
(888) 727-BECK
me@glennbeck.com

Jeff Katz Show (KNEW)
(800) 345-5639
jeffkatz@910knew.com

John and Ken Show (KFI)
(800) 520-1534
johnandken@johnandkenshow.com

Rick Roberts Show (KFMB)
(800) 760-KFMB
rickroberts@kfmb.com

Ronn Owens Show (KGO)
(415) 808-0810
emailronn@aol.com

Tom Sullivan Show (KFBK)
(916) 921-1530
tomsullivan@clearchannel.com

Colorado

Mike Rosen Show (KOA)
(303) 713-8585
mikerosen@clearchannel.com

Peter Boyles Show (KHOW)
(303) 713-TALK
peterboyles@clearchannel.com

Florida

Neil Rogers Show (WQAM)
(877) 785-NEIL
neilrogers@wqam.com
Russ Rollins Show (WTKS)
(888) 978-1041
russ@wtks.com

Todd Schnitt Show (WFLA)
(800) 801-8999
schnittshow@aol.com

Georgia

Martha Zoller Show (WDUN)
(800) 552-9386
martha@marthazoller.com

Illinois

Don Wade and Roma Show (WLS)
(312) 591-8900
via wlsam.com

Kathy and Judy Show (WGN)
(312) 591-7200
kathyomalley@wgnradio.com
judymarkey@wgnradio.com

Steve Dahl Show (WCKG)
(312) 591-9254
steve@dahl.com

Indiana

Greg Garrison Show (WIBC)
(317) 239-1070
ggarrison@indy.emmis.com

Iowa

Mickelson in the Morning (WHO)
w/Jan Mickelson
mickelson@netins.net

Kansas

Jerry Agar Show (KMBZ)
(913) 576-7798
jagar@entercom.com

Maryland

Chip Franklin Show (WBAL)
(800) 767-WBAL
chip@wbal.com

Les Kinsolving Show (WCBM)
(800) 922-6680
les@leskinsolving.com

Massachusetts

Big Show w/ Glen Ordway (WEEI)
(617) 779-0850
thebigshow@weei.com

Blute & Scotto (WRKO)
(617) 266-6868
bluteandscotto@wrko.com

Jay Severin Show (WTKK)
(617) 822-1969
ExtremeGames@969fmtalk.com

Michigan

Paul W. Smith Show (WJR)
(800) 859-0957
paul.w.smith@abc.com

Minnesota

Joe Soucheray Show (KSTP)
(651) 646-8255
gljoe@am1500.com

Nebraska

Drive Time Omaha with Tom
Becka (KFAB)
(800) 543-1110
becka@kfab.com

Nevada

(702) 889-React (7322)

Alan Stock w/Heidi
Harris (KXNT)
(702) 889-7322
via kxnt.com

New Jersey

Carton & Rossi Show (WKXW)
(800) 283-1015
CartonAndRossi@nj1015.com

New Mexico

Jim Villanucci Show (KKOB)
(800) 460-0770
jim@radiojim.com

New York

Curtis & Kuby in the Morning
(WABC)
(800) 848-9222
via WABCradio.com

Hunter and Malzberg Morning Show
(WWRL)
(212) 868-0975
producers@wwrl1600.com

Lionel (WOR)
(866) 6LIONEL
Lionel@Lionelonline.com

North Carolina

Kevin Miller Show (WPTF)
(919) 860-9783
kmiller@curtismedia.com

Maryland

Joe Madison Show (WOL)
(866) 801-TALK
lackeagle@joemadison.com

North Carolina

Jason Lewis Show (WBT)
(800) WBT-1110
jlewis@wbt.com

Ohio

Bill Cunningham Show (WLW)
(800) 843-2441
via WLW.com

Lincoln Ware Show (WDBZ)
(513)-749-1230
LWare@radio-one.com

Mike Trivisonno Show (WTAM)
(216) 578-1100
trivshow@wtam.com

Oregon

Tammy Bruce Show (Talk Radio)
(602) 277-1100
heytammybruce@yahoo.com

Pennsylvania

Dom Giordano Show (WPHT)
(215) 839-1210
domshow@aol.com

Drive In with Fred Honsberger
(KDKA)
(412) 333-5352
via kdkaradio.com

Michael Smerconish Show
(WPHT)
(215) 839-1210
webmail@mastalk.com

Rhode Island

Arlene Violet Show (WHJJ)
(866) 920-WHJJ
arleneviolet@clearchannel.com

Dan Yorke Show (WPRO)
(401) 437-0630
dan@630wpro.com

Tennessee

Phil Valentine Show (WWTN)
(615) 737-WWTN
Phil@PhilValentine.com

Steve Gill Mornings (WWTN)
(615) 737-9986
steve@gillreport.com

Texas

Ankarlo Mornings (KLIF)
(800) 583-1570
ankarlo@ankarlo.net

Jack Riccardi Show (KTSA)
(800) 299-KTSA
jack@ktsa.com

Mark Davis Show (WBAP)
(214) 787-1820
mdavis@wbap.com

Washington

Kirby Wilbur Show (KVI)
(888) 312-5757
kwilbur@fisherradio.com

Washington, D.C.

Alan Nathan Show
(Radio America)
n/a
anathan@radioamerica.com

Michael Graham Show (WMAL)
(888) 630-WMAL
michaelgraham@630wmal.com

Wisconsin

Belling & Company (WISN)
(414) 799-1130
markbelling@clearchannel.com

Green House w/ Jonathan Green
(WTMJ)
(800) 877-1620
greenhouse@620wtmj.com

Presidential Passivity Is Poison

Congress has a number of major tax reform bills before it. Here is the Congressional Research Service's update on who is proposing what. Nothing substantive will come to pass, however, without vigorous promotion by the president. Only he can fire up the public support necessary to overcome entrenched, special-interest opposition.

CRS Issue Brief for Congress
Received through the CRS Web

Flat Tax Proposals and Fundamental Tax Reform: An Overview

Updated March 23, 2005

James M. Bickley
Government and Finance Division

Congressional Research Service • The Library of Congress

CONTENTS

IB95060   03-23-05

Flat Tax Proposals and Fundamental Tax Reform: An Overview

SUMMARY

President George W. Bush has stated that tax reform is one of his top priorities in the 109th Congress. On January 7, 2005, he appointed a nine member bi-partisan panel to study the "complicated mess" posed by the federal tax code and to propose options to reform the code.

Consequently, the idea of replacing our current income tax system with a "flat-rate tax" is receiving renewed congressional interest. Although referred to as "flat-rate taxes," many of the recent proposals go much further than merely adopting a flat rate tax structure. Some involve significant income tax base broadening while others entail changing the tax base from income to consumption.

Proponents of these tax revisions are often concerned with simplifying the tax system, making the government less intrusive, and creating an environment more conducive to saving. Critics are concerned with the distributional consequences and transitional costs of a dramatic change in the tax system.

Most observers believe that the problems and complexities of our current tax system are not primarily related to the number of tax rates, but rather stem from difficulties associated with measuring the tax base.

Most of the recent tax reform proposals, such as the Shelby (S. 1040 in the 108th Congress), the English (H.R. 269 in the 108th Congress), the Specter (S. 907 in the 108th Congress), and the Tauzin (H.R. 4168 in the 108th Congress), would have changed the tax base from income to consumption. Some of these proposals are being reintroduced in the 109th Congress. As of March 21, 2005, the Linder proposal (H.R. 25) and the companion bill S. 25 (Chambliss) for a national sales tax have been introduced in the 109th Congress.

One or more of four major types of broad-based consumption taxes are included in these congressional tax proposals: the value-added tax (VAT), the retail sales tax, the consumed-income tax, and the flat tax based on a proposal formulated by Robert E. Hall and Alvin Rabushka of the Hoover Institution. In addition, Representative Fattah proposed (H.R. 3759 in the 108th Congress) that the Treasury conduct a study of the implementation of a transaction fee as a replacement for all existing federal taxes on individuals and corporations.

Other tax reform proposals focus on income as the base. The Gephardt proposal would keep income as the tax base but broaden the base and lower the tax rates. Representative Crane's proposal (H.R. 1789 in the 108th Congress) would have levied a tax on the earned income of each individual as a replacement for the current individual income tax, corporate income tax, and estate and gift tax. Representative Burgess' proposal (H.R. 1040 in the 109th Congress) would have permitted each taxpayer to choose between the current individual income tax or an alternative flat tax based on the Hall-Rabushka concept. Senator Dorgan's proposal would allow most taxpayers to choose between the current individual tax system and his "shortcut" tax plan under which taxes withheld would equal the employee's tax liability.

Congressional Research Service   •   The Library of Congress   CRS

IB95060   03-23-05

MOST RECENT DEVELOPMENTS

On March 2, 2005, Representative Michael Burgess introduced H.R. 1040, the Freedom Flat Tax Act. This bill would allow individuals to elect irrevocably to pay a flat tax as an alternative to our current income tax. In the first two years, the flat tax rate would be 19%, but in subsequent years the rate would decline to 17%.

BACKGROUND AND ANALYSIS

President George W, Bush has stated that tax reform is one of his top priorities in the 109th Congress. He has appointed a nine member bi-partisan panel to study the "complicated mess" posed by the federal tax code and to propose options to reform the code. Consequently, fundamental tax reform is a major legislative issue in the 109th Congress. Fundamental tax reform has been an important issue in prior Congresses, and many past bills are expected to be reintroduced. Most proposals for fundamental tax reform would change the tax base from income to consumption.

The Relationship Between Income and Consumption

Although our current tax structure is referred to as an income tax, it actually contains elements of both an income- and a consumption-based tax. For example, the current tax system includes in its tax base wages, interest, dividends, and capital gains, all of which are consistent with an income tax. At the same time, however, the current tax system excludes some savings, such as pension and Individual Retirement Account contributions, which is consistent with a tax using a consumption base.

The easiest way to understand the differences between the income and consumption tax bases is to define and understand the economic concept of income. In its broadest sense, income is a measure of the command over resources that an individual acquires during a given time period. Conceptually, individuals can exercise two options with regard to their income: they can consume it or they can save it. This theoretical relationship between income, consumption, and saving allows a very useful accounting identity to be established; income, by definition, must equal consumption plus saving. It follows that a tax that has a measure of comprehensive income applies to both consumption and savings. A consumption tax, however, applies to income minus saving.

A consumption tax can be levied at the individual level in a form very similar to the current system. An individual would add up all income in the same way as he or she does now under the income tax but then would subtract out net savings (saving minus borrowing). The result of these calculations would be the consumption base on which tax is assessed. Equivalently, a consumption tax can also be collected at the retail level in the form of a sales tax or at each stage of the production process in the form of a value-added tax (VAT).

Regardless of the form or point where a consumption tax is collected, it is ultimately paid by the individual doing the consuming. It should be noted that consumption, in the economy as a whole, is smaller than income. Thus, to raise equal amounts of revenue in a given year, tax rates on a comprehensive consumption base would have to be higher than the tax rates on a comprehensive income base.

What Should Be Taxed?

Should the tax base be income or consumption? Is one inherently superior to the other? How do they stack up in terms of simplicity, fairness, and efficiency — the three standards by which tax systems are generally assessed? There appears to be insufficient theoretical or empirical evidence to conclude that a consumption-based tax is inherently superior to an income-based tax or vice versa.

One issue associated with the choice of a tax base is equity — how the tax burden will be distributed across income classes and different types of taxpayers. For example, a tax is "progressive" if its burden rises as incomes rise. While some types of consumption taxes can be designed to achieve any desired level of progressivity with respect to consumption alone, their progressivity with respect to income could only be approximated. Also, a consumption tax would involve a redistribution of the tax burden by age group, with the young and old generally bearing more of the total tax burden than those in their prime earning years. And the transition from an income-based tax to a consumption-based tax would have the potential for creating windfall gains for some taxpayers and losses for others.

A definitive assessment cannot be made of the effects of taxing consumption on either economic efficiency or the aggregate level of savings. Although the current tax system's distortions of the relative attractiveness of present and future consumption (saving) would be eliminated, to raise the same amount of tax revenue, a consumption-based tax would require an increase in marginal tax rates (since consumption is smaller than income). This action, in turn, would increase the current system's distortion between the attractiveness of market (e.g. purchased products) and nonmarket activities (e.g. leisure). The net effect on overall economic efficiency cannot be ascertained theoretically. In addition, economic theory indicates a consumption tax would not necessarily produce an increase in saving. The increase in after tax income might reduce saving, while the increase in the return to saving may increase it; the net result is uncertain.

A positive aspect of a consumption-based tax is the ease with which the individual and corporate tax systems could be integrated. In addition, the problems introduced by separate provisions for capital gains, attempts to distinguish between real and nominal income, and depreciation procedures would essentially be eliminated. It is doubtful, however, that a consumption-based tax would have much effect on the complexities introduced into the system to promote specific social and economic goals. Many of the same factors that influenced the design of the current income tax system would exert the same influences on the final design of a consumption tax.

Whether one prefers income or consumption, one tax rate or multiple tax rates, a critical point to remember is that the benefits to be derived from tax revision would result from defining the tax base more comprehensively than it is under current law. A tax with a base that is comprehensively defined would prove more equitable and efficient than a tax with a less comprehensively defined base.

Types of Broad-Based Consumption Taxes

Four major types of broad-based consumption taxes are included in congressional tax proposals: the value-added tax (VAT), the retail sales tax, the consumed-income tax, and the flat tax based on a proposal formulated by Robert I. Hall and Alvin Rabushka of the Hoover Institution.

Value-Added Tax

A value-added tax is a tax, levied at each stage of production, on firms' value added. The value added of a firm is the difference between a firm's sales and a firm's purchases of inputs from other firms. The VAT is collected by each firm at every stage of production.

There are three alternative methods of calculating VAT: the credit method, the subtraction method, and the addition method. Under the credit method, the firm calculates the VAT to be remitted to the government by a two-step process. First, the firm multiplies its sales by the tax rate to calculate VAT collected on sales. Second, the firm credits VAT paid on inputs against VAT collected on sales and remits this difference to the government. The firm calculates its VAT liability before setting its prices to fully shift the VAT to the buyer. Under the credit-invoice method, a type of credit method, the firm is required to show VAT separately on all sales invoices and to calculate the VAT credit on inputs by adding all VAT shown on purchase invoices.

Under the subtraction method, the firm calculates its value added by subtracting its cost of taxed inputs from its sales. Next, the firm determines its VAT liability by multiplying its value added by the VAT rate. Under the addition method, the firm calculates its value added by adding all payments for untaxed inputs (e.g., wages and profits). Next, the firm multiplies its value added by the VAT rate to calculate VAT to be remitted to the government.

Retail Sales Tax

In contrast to a VAT, a retail sales tax is a consumption tax levied only at a single stage of production, the retail stage. The retailer collects a specific percentage markup in the retail price of a good or service which is then remitted to the tax authorities.

Consumed-Income Tax

Under this consumption tax, taxpayers would keep their assets in an account equivalent to a current IRA (individual retirement account). Net contributions to this account (contributions less withdrawals) would be deducted from income to determine the level of consumed-income. In contrast to a VAT or sales tax, policymakers would have the option of applying a progressive rate structure to the level of consumed-income. Each individual would be responsible for calculating his consumed-income and paying his tax obligation.

Flat Tax (Hall/Rabushka Concept)

A flat tax could be levied based on the proposal formulated by Robert E. Hall and Alvin Rabushka of the Hoover Institution. Their proposal would have two components: a wage tax and a cash-flow tax on businesses. (A wage tax is a tax only on salaries and wages; a cash-flow tax is generally a tax on gross receipts minus all outlays.) It is essentially a modified VAT, with wages and pensions subtracted from the VAT base and taxed at the individual level. Under a standard VAT, a firm would not subtract its wage and pension contributions when calculating its tax base. Under this proposal, some wage income would not be included in the tax base because of exemptions. Under a standard VAT, all wage income would be included in the tax base.

International Comparisons

There are two major distinctions between recent flat tax proposals for the United States that would change the tax base from income to consumption and the current tax systems of other developed nations. First, although the United States is the only developed nation without a broad-based consumption tax at the national level, other developed nations adopted broad-based consumption taxes as adjuncts to rather than as replacements for their income-based taxes. Most of the congressional proposals would replace our current income taxes with consumption taxes, rather than use consumption taxes as adjuncts to our current income-based system.

Second, all developed nations with VATs, except Japan, calculate their VATs using the credit-invoice method. Most of the current U.S. flat tax proposals, which include VAT components, however, would use the subtraction method of calculation.

Other Types of Fundamental Tax Reform

Two other types of fundamental tax reform are income tax reform and a tax plan that gives taxpayers a choice of systems.

Income Tax Reform: Base Broadening

Income tax base broadening would involve eliminating most tax preferences, increasing the standard deduction and personal exemption allowances, and reducing tax rates. House Minority Leader Gephardt's proposal is in this category.

Option of the Current or an Alternative Income Tax System

Two proposals would give taxpayers the option of either paying taxes under the current income tax or paying a flat rate income tax. Representative Burgess' proposal and Senator Dorgan's proposal are in this category.

Description of Selected Proposals

Numerous flat tax (or modified flat tax) proposals are receiving the most congressional attention. Some of the proposals (the Shelby, the English, the Specter, the Tauzin, and the Linder plans) would change the tax base from income to consumption. Representative Gephardt's proposal would keep income as the tax base. Representative Crane's proposal would levy a tax on the earned income of each individual as a replacement for the current individual income tax, corporate income tax, and estate and gift tax. Representative Burgess' proposal would allow each taxpayer to choose between the current individual income tax return and an alternative individual tax return with a flat rate. Senator Dorgan's proposal would allow most taxpayers to choose between the current individual tax system and his "shortcut" tax plan under which taxes withheld would equal the employee's tax liability. Representative Fattah's proposal would require that the Treasury conduct a study of the implementation of a transaction fee as a replacement for all existing federal taxes on individuals and corporations. While some of these plans are more detailed than others, none of the proposals has the level of detail that would be required to make a plan operational. Many difficult details and transitional considerations have yet to be addressed. Some proposals have been formulated into bills introduced in the 105th, 106th, 107th, 108th, or 109th Congresses. After the heading of each proposal, the most recent bill introduced is specified by its number.

The Shelby Proposal

S. 1040 in the 108th Congress. The Tax Simplification Act of 2003 proposed by Senator Shelby was modeled after the proposal formulated in 1981 by Hall and Rabushka. This flat tax would levy a consumption tax as a replacement for the individual and corporate income taxes, and the estate and gift taxes.

As noted above, this proposal would have two components: a wage tax and a cash-flow tax on businesses. It is essentially a modified VAT, with wages and pensions subtracted from the VAT base and taxed at the individual level. Under this proposal, some wage income would not be included in the tax base because of deductions, while under a VAT all wage income would be included in the tax base.

Initially the individual wage tax would be levied at a 19% rate, but when the tax was fully phased in, this rate would decline to 17%. The individual wage tax would be levied on all wages, salaries, pensions, and unemployment compensation. In addition, government employees and employees of nonprofit organizations would have to add to their wage tax base the imputed value of their fringe benefits.

The individual wage tax would not be levied on Social Security receipts. Thus, the current partial taxation of Social Security payments to high income households would be repealed. Social Security contributions would continue to be taxed; that is, they would not be deductible and would be made from after-tax income. Firms would pay the business tax on their Social Security contributions. Individuals would pay the wage tax on their Social Security contributions. The individual wage tax would have "standard deductions" that would equal the sum of the "basic standard deduction" and the "additional standard deduction."

The "basic standard deduction" would depend on filing status. For tax year 2003, the basic standard deduction would have been the following:

- $25,580 for a married couple filing jointly or a surviving spouse;
- $16,330 for a single head of household;
- $12,790 for a single person; and
- $12,790 for a married person filing a separate return.

The "additional standard deduction" would be an amount equal to $5,510 times the number of dependents of the taxpayer.

All deductions would be indexed for inflation using the consumer price index (CPI).

Initially businesses would pay a tax of 19% (declining to 17% when the tax was fully phased in after December 31, 2004) on the difference (if positive) between gross revenue and the sum of purchases from other firms, wage payments, and pension contributions. This business tax would cover corporations, partnerships, and sole proprietorships. Pension contributions would be deductible but there would be no deductions for fringe benefits. In addition, state and local taxes (including income taxes) and payroll taxes would not be deductible.

Activities of government entities and tax-exempt organizations would be exempt from the business tax.

If the business's aggregate deductions exceed gross revenue, then the excess of aggregate deductions can be carried forward to the next year and increased by a percentage equal to the three-month Treasury rate for the last month of the taxable year.

Any congressional action that raises taxes would require a three-fifth (supermajority) in both the Senate and the House of Representatives.

The English Proposal

H.R. 269 in the 108th Congress. This proposal of Representative English (Simplified USA Tax) was based on the Domenici-Nunn proposal. The *corporate income tax* would be replaced by a cash-flow business tax (a subtraction-method VAT). The gross tax base (value-added) would equal gross receipts less purchases from other firms. The tentative tax would be determined by multiplying the value-added by the appropriate tax rate. A tax rate of 8% would apply to the first $150,000 of a business' value-added, and a tax rate of 12% would apply to all of the business's value-added over $150,000. A business tax rate of 12% would apply to all imports. A credit for the 7.65% employer-paid OASDHI payroll tax (commonly called FICA or the Social Security tax) would be subtracted from the tentative tax to calculate the business's tax liability for the year.

The *individual income tax* would be replaced by a tax on consumed-income. An individual's tax liability would be calculated by (1) calculating gross income, (2) subtracting exemptions and deductions, (3) applying a progressive rate structure to the difference, and (4) subtracting a credit for the 7.65% employer-paid OASDHI payroll tax payments. Gross income would equal wages and salaries plus interest, dividends, pension receipts, and amounts received from the sale of stock and other assets. Deductions would be allowed for charitable contributions, home mortgage interest, and higher education tuition. Deductions would also be allowed for retirement-oriented 401(k) contributions and IRAs for lower income families.

The Simplified USA Tax eliminates the double taxation of savings by allowing everyone to contribute after-tax income to a USA Roth IRA, which is a universal savings vehicle. After five years, accumulated principal and earnings on principal can be withdrawn on a tax-free basis at any time and for any purpose. The federal estate and gift tax would be repealed.

The Specter Proposal

S. 907 in the 108th Congress. The Flat Tax Act proposed by Senator Specter also was modeled after the Hall-Rabushka proposal and thus is similar to that of Senator Shelby. The Specter flat rate consumption tax would replace the federal individual and corporate income taxes and the federal estate and gift taxes.

This proposal would have two components: a wage tax and a cash-flow tax on businesses. It is essentially a modified VAT, with wages, salaries, and pensions subtracted from the VAT base and taxed at the individual level.

The individual wage tax would be levied at a 20% rate on all wages, salaries, and pensions. In addition, government employees and employees of nonprofits would have to add to their wage base the imputed value of their fringe benefits. The individual wage tax would have "standard deductions" that would equal the sum of the "basic standard deduction" and the "additional standard deduction."

The "basic standard deduction" would depend on filing status. For tax year 2004, the basic standard deduction would be the following:

- $17,500 for a joint return;
- $17,500 for a surviving spouse;
- $15,000 for a head of household;
- $10,000 for a married taxpayer filing separately; and
- $10,000 for a single taxpayer.

The "additional standard deduction" would be an amount equal to $5,000 times the number of dependents of the taxpayer. All deductions would be indexed for inflation.

Individuals would be allowed to deduct up to $2,500 ($1,250 in the case of a married individual filing a separate return) annually for charitable contributions. Individuals also would be allowed to deduct "qualified residence interest" on acquisition indebtedness not exceeding $100,000 ($50,000 in the case of a married individual filing a separate return).

The business tax would be levied at a 20% tax rate on gross revenue less the sum of purchases from other firms, wage payments, pension contributions, and the cost of personal and real property used in the business. Purchases from other firms would include capital goods. If the business's aggregate deductions exceed gross revenue, then the excess of aggregate deductions can be carried forward to the next year and increased by a percentage equal to the three-month Treasury rate for the last month of the taxable year.

This tax reform act would have become operational on January 1, 2004.

The Tauzin Proposal

H.R. 4168 in the 108th Congress. This proposal would replace the personal and corporate income taxes, estate and gift taxes and all non-trust dedicated excise taxes with a 15% national retail sales tax. Each qualified family unit would receive a sales tax rebate equal to the product of the sales tax rate and the lesser of the poverty level (adjusted for the number of dependents claimed) or the wage income of the family unit. The rebate amount would be included in each paycheck for that pay period. Any business required to collect and remit the sales tax would keep 0.5% of tax receipts to offset compliance costs. Any state choosing to do so could administer, collect and enforce the sales tax. To qualify as an "administering state," a state would have to conform its sales tax base to the federal base. Administering states could retain an administration fee equal to 1% of the amounts otherwise required to be remitted to the United States. A super majority vote of two-thirds of both Houses of Congress would be necessary to raise the sales tax rate or to create any exemptions to the sales tax.

The Linder Proposal

H.R. 25 in the 109th Congress. [A companion bill, S. 25, has been introduced in the 109th Congress by Senator Chambliss]. This proposal introduced by Representative Linder would repeal the individual income tax, the corporate income tax, all payroll taxes, the self-employment tax, and the estate and gift taxes and levy a 23% national retail sales tax as a replacement. Every family would receive a rebate of the sales tax on spending up to the federal poverty level (plus an extra amount to prevent any marriage penalty). The Social Security Administration would provide a monthly sales tax rebate to registered qualified families. The 23% national retail sales would not be levied on exports. The sales tax would be separately stated and charged. Social Security and Medicare benefits would remain the same with payroll tax revenue replaced by some of the revenue from the retail sales tax. States could elect to collect the national retail sales tax on behalf of the federal government in exchange for a fee. Taxpayers rights provisions are incorporated into the act.

The Gephardt Proposal

H.R. 3620 in the 105th Congress. Unlike most proposals, this proposal would reform the current income tax base rather than changing to a consumption base. The taxable income base for individuals under this proposal included all items of income currently taxed (salaries and wages, investment income, capital gains, business profit or loss, etc.) plus employee fringe benefits (other than health insurance), employer pension plan contribution, and tax-exempt state and local interest. Social Security benefits would be included to the same limited extent as they are under current law. Deductions from gross income (called "above-the-line" deductions, as distinct from the itemized deductions taken from adjusted gross income) would be allowed for alimony paid, one-half of the self-employment tax, investment interest, and job-related expenses. The only itemized deduction allowed would be home mortgage interest. Since pension contributions would be taxable, an exclusion would be allowed from pension income for the previously taxed contributions, the way annuities are taxed under current law. Accumulated earnings under pension plans, IRAs, and life insurance policies would remain tax-deferred, as under current law. The only credits allowed would be the earned income tax credit (EITC) and the foreign tax credit.

The standard deduction and personal exemption allowances would be increased and tax rates would be decreased from current law. In addition, the "marriage tax penalty" arising from these factors would be eliminated by making the joint filer allowances and tax brackets exactly twice those of a single filer. "Head-of-household" filers, which are single individuals with dependent children, would receive allowances and the first two tax brackets halfway in between the amounts for single and joint taxpayers; the higher tax brackets are equal the single-filer brackets. There would be no separate tax rates for capital gains.

The tax-free allowances would be:

- $9,000 for a joint return;
- $6,600 for a head of household;
- $4,500 for an individual; in addition
- $2,900 for each personal exemption.

The tax rate schedule would be:

- 10% marginal rate: married (joint) $0-$46,000; head of household $0-$32,000; single $0-$23,000.

- 20% marginal rate: married (joint) $46,000-$80,000; head of household $32,000-$40,000; single $23,000-$40,000.

- 26% marginal rate: married (joint) $80,000-$150,000; head of household $40,000-$75,000; single $40,000-$75,000.

- 32% marginal rate: married (joint) $150,000-$275,000; head of household $75,000-$137,500; single $75,000-$137,000.

- 34% marginal rate: married (joint) over $275,000; head of household over $137,500; single over $137,500.

This proposal would reduce "corporate welfare" by more than $50 billion. The plan apparently retains payroll and other taxes as under the current system. The plan is said to be revenue-neutral, to allow a post-card sized tax return for some taxpayers, and to require no return at all for over one-half of individual taxpayers. It also would stipulate that future changes in tax rates could be made only by national referendum.

The Crane Proposal

H.R. 1789 in the 108th Congress. This proposal would repeal the corporate income tax, the individual income tax, the estate and gift tax, and replace these taxes with a flat rate tax of 10% on individuals' earned income. The first $10,000 in earned income would be exempt from taxation. This exemption level would be indexed for changes in the consumer price index. Earned income would be defined as the sum of wages, salaries, and other employee compensation; the amount of the taxpayer's net earnings from self-employment; and the amount of dividends that are from a personal service corporation or that are otherwise directly or indirectly compensation for services. Fringe benefits included in earned income would be valued at the cost to the employer. This proposal would establish an amnesty for all prior tax liability attributable to legal activities.

The Dorgan Proposal

S. 551 in the 107th Congress. Under the "Fair and Simple Shortcut Tax Plan," most employees would be allowed to provide employers with additional information on their W-4 (deduction) Form. For example, whether the employee is a homeowner. Single taxpayers earning up to $50,000 in annual wage income (and with nonwage income of up to $2,500) and married couples filing jointly with up to $100,000 in annual wage income (and with nonwage income of up to $5,000) could choose a "shortcut" tax plan. The employer would file the W-4 Forms with the federal government. The employer would compute family deductions, factor in a deductions for home mortgage interest and property taxes, and determine the amount of federal income tax to withhold by taking 15% of wages after deductions less the child care credit. Under this "shortcut" plan, the amount of tax withheld would equal the employee's tax liability, and consequently, the employee would not have to file a tax return. If the employee calculated that their tax liability would be less under the current income tax, she or he would have the option of filling out and filing a tax return rather than paying tax under the "shortcut" plan. Senator Dorgan stated that up to 70 million taxpayers would be relieved from having to file a yearly federal individual income tax return.

Senator Dorgan's proposal would make five other changes in the current tax code. First, the first $1 million in self-employment income would be exempt from the alternative minimum tax (AMT). Second, a taxpayer, who cannot use the shortcut method, would be allowed a tax credit for 50% of the costs (maximum of $200) of paying a preparer if the tax return is filed electronically. Third, during the first year to cover start-up costs, a business would be allowed a tax credit equal to the lesser of $1,000 or 50% of the costs of complying with the exact withholding option. Fourth, the marriage penalty would be reduced by making the standard deduction for married couples filing jointly double the amount available for single filers. Fifth, taxpayers would be offered a substantial incentive for savings and investment by exempting from taxation up to $500 of dividend and interest income for an individual and up to $1,000 for a couple.

The Burgess Proposal

H.R. 1040 in the 109th Congress. This proposal would allow taxpayers to select a flat tax as an alternative to the current income tax system. The flat tax was based on the concepts of Hall-Rabushka and is similar to the Armey flat tax proposal. The individual's selection of the flat tax would be irrevocable. In the first two years, the flat tax rate would be 19%, and in subsequent years it would fall to 17%. An individual engaged in a business activity may elect irrevocably, as an alternative to our current income tax system, to be taxed on business taxable income that equals gross sales less the cost of business inputs for business activity, wages, and retirement contributions. For the first two years, a 19% rate would apply to business taxable income, but after the first two years, this rate would decline to 17%. This act would have become effective for tax year 2006.

The Fattah Proposal

H.R. 3759 in the 108th Congress. This proposal would require the Secretary of the Treasury to conduct an in-depth study of the implementation of a transaction fee as a replacement for all existing federal taxes on individuals and corporations. This transaction fee would apply to all cash and non-cash transactions (including checks, credit cards, transfers of stocks, bonds, and other financial instruments). The fee would not apply to cash transactions of less than $500, and salaries and wages paid by employers to employees. The fee would be double, or higher than, the standard transaction fee on cash withdrawals from financial institutions. The fee would be collected by the seller or financial institution servicing the transaction. The fee would be set at least at the level to replace revenues generated under the Internal Revenue Code. A higher fee could be levied to pay for one or more of the following: elimination of the national debt over 10 years, a federal revenue sharing program with the states to support 50% of the K-16 education costs, a federal health care program providing insurance coverage for the estimated 43 million uninsured Americans, and a federal revenue sharing program supporting community and economic development investments in high poverty areas. The Secretary of the Treasury would submit to Congress the results of the study in a comprehensive analytical report not later than one year after the enactment of this act.

LEGISLATION

H.R. 25 (Linder). Fair Tax Act of 2005. To promote freedom, fairness, and economic opportunity by repealing the income tax and other taxes, abolishing the Internal Revenue Service, and enacting a national sales tax to be administered primarily by the States. Introduced January 4, 2005; referred to the Committee on Ways and Means.

H.R. 1040 (Burgess). Freedom Flat Tax Act. This bill would allow individuals to elect irrevocably to pay a flat tax as an alternative to our current income tax. In the first two years, the flat tax rate would be 19%, but in subsequent years the rate would decline to 17%. This bill would become effect in tax year 2006. Introduced March 2, 2005; referred to the Committee on Ways and Means.

S. 25 (Chambliss). Fair Tax Act of 2005. To promote freedom, fairness, and economic opportunity by repealing the income tax and other taxes, abolishing the Internal Revenue Service, and enacting a national sales tax to be administered primarily by the states. Introduced January 24, 2005; referred to the Senate Finance Committee.

FOR ADDITIONAL READING

CRS Products

CRS Report RL30351. *Consumption Taxes and the Level and Composition of Saving*, by Steven Maguire.

CRS Report RL32603. *The Flat Tax and National Sales Tax: Overview of the Issues*, by Gregg A. Esenwein and Jane G. Gravelle.

CRS Report RL32266. *Transaction Tax: General Overview*, by Maxim Shvedov.

CRS Issue Brief IB91078. *Value-Added Tax as a New Revenue Source*, by James M. Bickley.

CRS Issue Brief IB92069. *A Value-Added Tax Contrasted with a National Sales Tax*, by James M. Bickley.

Killing the Death Tax

Abolishing the death tax has widespread public and congressional backing. The exaction does immense harm as this article succinctly, lucidly lays out.

National Review
November 25, 2002, Monday
"Death and Taxes: The Political Fortunes of the Estate Tax"
By Ramesh Ponnuru

No policy of the Bush administration has drawn more withering scorn than its drive to eliminate the estate tax. In opposing the tax, Bush "kowtow[s] to plutocrats" and displays "willful obtuseness." That's the verdict of Andrew Sullivan—and he's one of the most pro-Bush pundits around.

For *New York Times* columnist Paul Krugman, the fact that only the top 2 percent of estates pay the tax means that the campaign against it is "[t]he most remarkable example of how politics has shifted in favor of the wealthy." Marshall Wittmann, another commentator, said the campaign was one of the reasons he left the Republican party this year. Conservative economist Irwin Stelzer has argued in *The Weekly Standard* that the estate tax serves the public good by promoting meritocracy. That's Sullivan's view, too.

Trying to abolish the estate tax does not, in short, win rave reviews on op-ed pages. But there is a strong case for abolition. What's more, abolition is popular. It's not a favor Republicans do for their contributors behind closed doors. Norm Coleman, Jim Talent, and John Thune—the three candidates the GOP touted all year as its best shots at picking up Senate seats—all trumpeted their opposition to the tax and accused their opponents of supporting it.

It's true that opposing the estate tax wins the Republicans support from some powerful lobbies: the National Restaurant Association, the National Beer Wholesalers Association, and the Farm Bureau, to name a few. But repeal also has broad and deep support from voters. In May, the Democratic polling firm Greenberg Quinlan Rosner found that 60 percent of likely voters favored repeal, with 43 percent saying they "strongly" favored it. (The only silver lining for Democrats is that voters preferred "reform" to repeal, once exposed to a series of arguments for that position.) Wittmann aside, the issue seems to be winning votes for the GOP.

Under the terms of the Bush tax cut, the estate tax is scheduled to be slowly phased out over the course of the decade. But then the tax cut expires, so the estate tax comes back in full force in 2011. Republicans are pushing to make estate-tax repeal permanent. In June, 41 House Democrats broke ranks to vote for permanent repeal. Eleven Senate Democrats—more than a fifth of Tom Daschle's caucus—voted for a resolution supporting permanent abolition.

While campaigning for re-election, Sen. Tim Johnson, a South Dakota Democrat, said he supports repeal (even though he actually voted against making repeal permanent). Democratic senator Mary Landrieu ran an ad that told Louisianans that "[s]he...voted eleven times to abolish the death tax."

Those Democrats who oppose repeal hasten to explain that they favor estate-tax relief. The estate tax currently exempts estates smaller than $675,000, and these Democrats would raise that exemption. Even the late Paul Wellstone took this tack in his re-election campaign. Estate-tax opponents, however, regard the exemption proposals as a dodge. Most of them build on an existing provision of estate-tax law that is so complicated that almost nobody ever gets exempted.

The debate over the estate tax is typically framed as a question of justice. Democrats say it is unfair to give a tax break to the super-rich or to reward their idle heirs. Republicans say it is unfair to tax the wealth that a person has accumulated over a lifetime, especially since he paid income taxes while earning it. The economic impact of the tax is at best a secondary issue. But it was concern about that impact that brought the issue before Congress in the first place.

Like other tax-policy ideas that infuriate liberals, the campaign against the estate tax originated with Arthur Laffer. In 1992, congressman Chris Cox called the famed supply-side economist and asked what tax cut would deliver the most economic bang for the buck. Laffer said getting rid of the estate tax would be at the top of his list.

The economic case against the tax is pretty simple. Being able to pass on wealth to one's children is a strong incentive for wealth accumulation. By reducing that incentive, the estate tax reduces saving and investment. Republican staffers at Congress's Joint Economic Committee estimated in 1998 that the effect of the estate tax has been to reduce America's capital stock by half a trillion dollars.

Liberals underestimate the cost of the estate tax by looking only at the 2 percent of estates that pay it. The tax generates costs for non-payers too. It's a major source of complexity in the tax code. The National Association of Manufacturers reports that 40 percent of its members have spent more than $100,000 each on estate-tax planning. The complexity of the tax also means that it is levied less on the basis of the size of a man's estate than on the shrewdness of his estate planners. In the late 1990s, estates worth between $2.5 and $5 million dollars that paid the tax actually paid a higher average tax rate than estates worth more than $20 million that paid it.

The tax forces the breakup of cash-poor family businesses. It does not appear to do much to promote economic equality, and it may even make inequality of consumption worse since it encourages the elderly rich to spend their money.

Is the estate tax nevertheless necessary to raise funds for the federal government? No. The estate tax brought in $26.5 billion—around 1.4 percent of federal revenues—last year. And that's an overestimate. In the 1980s, Stanford economist B. Douglas Bernheim concluded that because of its wealth-destroying effects, the estate tax probably caused federal revenues to be lower than they would be without the tax. Needless to say, the pro-tax pundits do not grapple with the possibility that the estate tax is a revenue loser.

But other economists do not regard the charge as outlandish. Indeed, important aspects of the foregoing case against the estate tax have been endorsed by many prominent liberal economists—notably Clinton administration officials Alicia Munnell, Alan Blinder, and Joseph Stiglitz.

Cox was convinced that the estate tax hurts the economy. He also believed repeal was a real possibility. His home state of California had eliminated most of its estate taxes in a 1982 referendum, which passed by a landslide. In 1993, he introduced his bill to eliminate the estate tax federally.

Outside Congress, his ally was Jim Martin, the head of 60 Plus, a conservative seniors group. It was Martin who came up with the idea of relabeling the estate tax "the death tax." The phrase is a little misleading, since estate taxes hit only those who leave estates rather than everyone who dies. But Martin's rhetoric was politically brilliant, as it made the tax seem especially cruel. "Dying should not be a taxable event," he says.

In 1995, freshman Republican senator Jon Kyl of Arizona introduced Cox's House bill in his chamber. Cox, meanwhile, slowly built up co-sponsors. By 1996 there were 102; by 1998, 204.

The insurance industry has lobbied hard against repeal because it sells products designed to soften the blow of the tax. Non-profits, especially universities, believe the estate tax encourages donations. Ideological liberals have also tried to fight repeal.

But it's congressional budget rules that have kept the estate tax alive. Complying with them forced Republicans to opt for the slow phase-out followed by a revived estate tax, rather than an immediate and permanent repeal. The effect has been to make the tax code more complex rather than simpler, and estate planning harder rather than easier.

But Cox and his allies will eventually prevail—and not because the super-rich have hoodwinked large swathes of the public, as Krugman posits. The campaign to repeal the estate tax reflects deep currents in American life, albeit ones that make liberals uncomfortable. Americans don't like taxes and tend to want them eliminated if possible. They don't resent the ability of wealthy people to give their fortunes to their kids. The day the estate tax expires for good is coming.

Good Intentions— Sickening Consequences

Health care has been immeasurably harmed by the federal income tax code. A corporate tax break meant to expand the availability of health insurance has perversely left tens of millions of people uninsured and disastrously inflated health care costs. But, as you will see here, help— including the flat tax—is on the way.

By Steve Forbes

Why do we have a health care crisis? Why are costs rising so rapidly? Basically because of the way we pay for health care. Change that and we would get the best of all worlds—better care and more accessible care *at less cost*.

Right now most health care bills are paid by third parties, such as employers or government. When you go to a doctor or hospital, you probably don't ask the price of a procedure or service you're seeking. If you did, the providers would assume you didn't have insurance. Price is the concern of the insurer, not you. Yet in every other part of our economy, you want to know what something costs in advance. Obviously, in the case of a health emergency, you're going to want the necessary care for you, your child, or loved one as quickly as possible. But most medical transactions are not of an acute emergency nature.

Health Savings Accounts (HSAs) were created in 2003 but are only beginning to take hold. HSAs are similar to Individual Retirement Accounts (IRAs)—but they are even better. Money goes into your HSA tax-free, it grows tax-free and can be spent on medical services or devices tax-free.

Under an HSA plan, an account is set up in the individual's name. The employer and/or you, the employee, deposit funds in that account. There are various rules on the maximum amount that can be put in each year. Money grows tax-free and can be used to pay your medical expenses. If you use up the fund in the account, then—and only then— do you face a deductible. If your health care expenses go above that deductible, then the catastrophic insurance coverage kicks in. HSAs thus put you, the consumer—the patient—in charge of more of your health care expenses.

With you, the consumer, in charge, we'll get the same kind of bene-fits in health care that we get for other goods and services—that is, more for less.

Recall what has happened to laser surgery for the eyes. Millions of people have had this procedure so that they no longer have to wear eye-glasses (although it doesn't always correct presbyopia, which is why peo-ple wear bifocals). Incredibly, the procedure today costs about a third of what it did ten years ago. Why? Because it's not covered by most health insurance plans. Since consumers want better value, providers find ways to provide this surgery at less cost. The same phenomenon has occurred with plastic surgery. Unless it is needed to deal with a disease or accident, plastic surgery is not covered by traditional health care insurance plans. If you want it, you comparison shop, finding out what various doctors charge for a specific procedure. Thus, plastic surgery costs have not experienced the kind of inflation that afflicts the rest of health care.

Health insurance is much cheaper when it carries a high deductible. HSAs enable individuals and businesses to buy these high-deductible plans and cover the bulk of the deductible with tax-free dollars. The total cost of health insurance and medical care will be lower for families and individuals who must buy policies directly and for businesses that provide them for their workers.

That's certainly been our experience at Forbes. Since the early 1990s, we have provided our people with variations on what are now called Health Savings Accounts. Each year we give each employee $2,000 for medical expenses. What you don't use is rolled over. If your costs exceed $2,000, then, and only then, do you face a deductible. At Forbes, each employee's deductible is based on his or her salary. We think it's preposterous that there should be a similar deductible for everyone. Deductibles should be based on each person's ability to pay, roughly 1% of salary. If an employee's medical costs exceed the deductible and the $2,000, then the catastrophic health insurance kicks in.

Over time, Forbes's health care costs have gone up far less than those of our peers. *Individuals get more value for their health care dollars than we as employers possibly could.*

An HSA has the wonderful benefit of individual ownership. It belongs to you, not your employer or the Washington politicians. Remember, at the end of a year, all funds in an HSA are rolled over. This is unlike so-called flexible spending accounts, which a number of companies offer these days. With a flex account, if you don't spend the money by year's end, you lose it. With HSAs, if you don't use the money, it remains in your account. It continues to grow tax-free. Owners of HSAs can thus accumulate significant balances that can be withdrawn tax-free for health care-related expenses. Even people with chronic illnesses benefit—they can acquire coverage under these plans and have most of their deductible paid for.

Since HSAs are owned by employees, not employers, they are fully portable. When you leave a company, the HSA goes with you. It's yours. And there's no need to suffer a lapse in health care coverage.

Consider the example of Whole Foods Market, Inc., a thriving grocery chain that employs more than 30,000 people. Whole Foods recently adopted a plan that puts its employees in charge of their health care. Employees don't have to pay premiums for high-deductible insurance, and Whole Foods kicks in $300 to $1,800 (based on an employee's tenure) to help defray the cost of the deductible.

Participation in Whole Foods' health program jumped from 65% to 95% in just one year, and Whole Foods' costs remained constant. At the end of 2003, the first year the plan was in effect, employees rolled over $14 million that was left in their savings accounts. So Whole Foods' health care costs remained constant while the cost of health care insurance in the U.S. increased an average of 13.9% over this same period. Remember, this happened with employees in control of their health care dollars, and they ended up with $14 million more in total assets because of the balances left in their accounts.

It's a plan that encourages responsibility by lowering costs as it rewards individuals and families who get better value for their money.

HSAs thus put downward pressure on escalating health care costs precisely because most health care consumers strive to get the most value for their money.

Misery Begets Misery

Forbes *pioneered the Tax Misery & Reform Index with global tax expert Jack Anderson. It graphically portrays just how onerous various countries' tax burdens truly are. Tax misery leads to economic misery—a lesson learned by a growing number of central and eastern European nations that have adopted the flat tax.*

"Flat and Happy"
By Jack Anderson

Our annual capitalist tool-kit to global taxation shows rates coming down—and getting flatter.

Flat-tax momentum is the big fiscal policy story of the year in much of Europe, with potential fallout in the U.S. Increasingly, entrepreneurial capitalists and skilled talent are in the driver's seat, able to move their activities to an ever wider range of places to do business. No wonder that high-tax fiefdoms like France and Sweden are feeling besieged.

In late March the present chief executive officer of Intel, Paul Otellini, told a U.S. presidential panel on tax reform that his biggest worry in deciding where in the world to build and operate a semi-conductor chip factory is *taxes*. They represent 20 percent of the almost $7 billion, ten-year build-and-operate cost for Intel.

Forbes's 2005 Misery & Reform Index shows more countries decreasing marginal rates than hiking them, a five-year trend.

In the mid-1990s, about the time U.S. reform advocates (including the editor-in-chief of this magazine) picked up on a flat-tax notion tried successfully in Hong Kong for decades, the newly free Baltics and central Europe put the idea into practice. Then, ironically, it took root in Russia, thanks to U.S. Tax Court Judge David Laro, a consultant to Moscow. By lowering and flattening marginal rates, these states are counterintuitively increasing their total tax revenues through better compliance and economic expansion.

Now it could be America's turn, under a plan put forward to George W. Bush's tax reform commission. The brainchild of Yale Law professor Michael Graetz, it would have a flat 25 percent tax on married couples with gross income in excess of $100,000 and singles with gross income above $50,000. The flat corporate tax rate would be reduced to the same 25 percent. A 14 percent value-added (consumption) tax, with special rates for food and medical needs, is a part of the plan and would be applied to imports but not to exports (achieving trade aims but skirting treaty problems).

To see the effect, check out the "U.S.A. (with reform)" entry in the Misery Index.

Meantime high-tax France is doing its part—at least for expatriates it wants to attract along with capital investment. A new law has eased French misery for expats by exempting many of the allowances beyond salary and bonus they typically receive from employers. Thanks to this, a $200,000-a-year executive moving from Chicago would cost his company $390,000 to maintain the same standard of living in Paris, about the same as in other continental business cities and far less than in London ($534,000). At a $500,000 pay level, the gap grows in Paris's favor. See the figures from ORC Worldwide location counselors at forbes.com/extra.

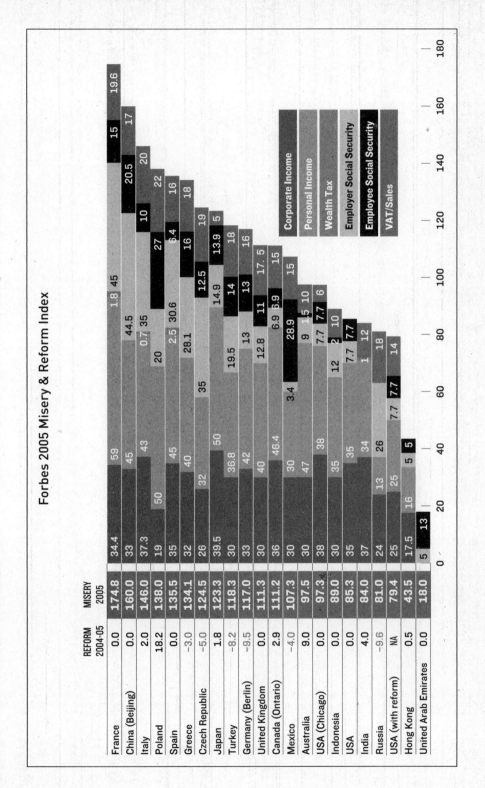

Forbes 2005 Misery & Reform Index

What Works?

Each year, numerous publications, including Forbes, *give taxpayers tips on what to do and not do to ease their tax burdens. Here are some common sense suggestions, published in* Forbes's *April 11, 2005, edition.*

By Janet Novack

You don't want to go to jail. You don't want to pay penalties. But you also don't want to pay more tax than you have to—it's not the American way. And your sister-in-law, your golf buddy, or your business partner is touting a "your CPA doesn't know this, but" way to pay less. How can you tell a legal tax dodge from an iffy of bad one?

The pat answer—if it sounds too good to be true, it probably is—isn't bad advice, but isn't always enough. Some things that sound too good to be true are allowed because Congress uses the tax code as an ersatz spending program; for example, if you invest in certain rental housing for low income folks, you can claim a special credit that isn't subject to the limitations imposed on losses from other passive activities.

Other improbable-sounding ploys work because the courts have blessed some taxpayer-friendly interpretation of a complicated code. Provided you do it right, you can chop your family's gift and estate taxes using family limited partnerships and grantor-retained annuity trusts.

For most taxpayers the best shelters are still the mundane ones: homes, retirement accounts, and stocks. Interest on up to $1 million in mortgage debt is deductible, and the first $500,000 in capital gains per couple from the sale of a primary home is tax free. For 2005 a worker can divert up to $14,000 ($18,000 for those 50 or older) into a tax-deferred 401(k). The gift-tax exclusion—$11,000 a year to each of as many different relatives and friends as you want—still works.

Want to get fancier? Here are some pointers to keep you safe:

1. Never agree to keep a tax dodge confidential. This is often a marker of a questionable shelter and limits your ability to run it by a dis-interested lawyer or accountant. The tax code may seem incompre-hensible to a normal person, but it's a public document; most legitimate strategies are well-known to tax pros.

2. Get that independent opinion. If you rely on a legal opinion pro-vided by a firm affiliated with the adviser who recommends a shelter, you could get stuck paying penalties as well as back taxes and interest if it doesn't work. Getting a pro's blessing can save you from penalties-if the pro is independent.

3. Don't pay outsize fees or fees that represent a percentage of taxes saved. Tax lawyers and CPAs can be expensive, but they charge by the hour. Watch out, too, for promoters who guarantee a fee refund if you don't get the desired tax result-the IRS considers this a marker of a suspect shelter.

4. Don't sign misleading or backdated documents. Abusive shelters often involve a series of transactions that were supposedly under-taken for nontax reasons. The taxpayer is asked to sign a letter claiming he made moves for business reasons, when those moves were really orchestrated by a promoter.

5. Be wary of charity-related shelters. There are some great tax-savvy ways to give to charity, such as contributing appreciated stock. But steer clear of any scheme that suggests charitable contributions can be used for your own benefit (say, reimbursing you for volunteer work you perform during retirement) or that involves claiming inflated deductions for noncash contributions. Promoters have moved into this area, and the IRS and Congress are now responding with crackdowns.

6. Stay onshore. Avoid schemes that promise secrecy through offshore entities. You must report foreign accounts worth $10,000 or more to the IRS; failing to do so is a criminal offense and one the IRS, thanks to new information-sharing agreements with other countries, may uncover.

7. Ignore claims that "none of my clients has been audited for this." It's irrelevant, even when true. The IRS has traditionally been slow to catch up with schemes, although it's speeding up. If the IRS really approves of some new strategy, in most cases you can get a "private letter ruling" from it saying so-for a fee.

8. Give extra scrutiny to ploys that combine different legitimate tax-favored entities to produce outsized results Congress didn't intend. Recent combo schemes the IRS has branded abusive couple S corporations with ESOPs and S corps with tax-exempt entities, such as public pension plans.

9. Don't make deals with your own IRAs or retirement accounts. There are stiff penalties for such "prohibited transactions." In one abusive scheme business owners sold their receivables for less than fair value to a shell company owned by their Roth IRAs-thus pumping excess money into the tax-free Roths.

10. Use the Web. Fraud-busting sites, such as quatloos.com, enable you to read up on the latest questionable schemes. At irs.gov you'll find a rundown on "listed" shelters-high-end strategies such as Son of Boss that the government says don't work-plus information on the latest lower-end scams, from "corporation soles" to flaky constitutional arguments on why the income tax isn't legal. Remember, however, that scam promoters have some pretty smart-looking Web pages, too.

Obligatory Maximum Tax

Although some of the details have changed, the essence of this
2002 Forbes *cover article on the increasingly rapacious,*
evermore encompassing Alternative Minimum Tax, remains true.

Forbes
April 1, 2002
"Killer Tax"
By Ashlea Ebeling and Janet Novack

The only good news: You can mitigate the damage. The alternative minimum tax was supposed to get the fat cats, but now millions of ordinary citizens are paying it—and Congress is addicted to the revenue. The only good news is that you can mitigate the damage.

Carl Wysocki, a retired Sun Microsystems finance manager in Scotts Valley, Calif., was caught in the web when he started diversifying his portfolio. Diane LeBeau, a New Bedford, Mass. nurse, was nailed for having too many children. Harold Nicholas, a Petersburg, N.Y. X-ray machine repairman, was punished for paying job expenses like gasoline bills out of his income; he'd have been safe if he had been reimbursed.The alternative minimum tax, created in 1969 after the revelation that a few hundred very wealthy Americans were paying no income tax at all, was aimed at the fat-cat class—people with tax shelters like oil wells and railcar leases. It has morphed into a monster that devours the middle class. Typical victims are like these three unfortunates—people whose "shelters" consist of doing innocuous things like cashing in employee stock options, having large families, running small businesses, living in high-tax California or New York City, or running up doctor bills. In the current tax season 1.7 million returns will be hit by the AMT. For the 2002 tax year 2.4 million taxpayers will pay more because of the AMT. By 2005 the AMT will claim 13.4 million victims— including 79% of taxpayers grossing $200,000 to $500,000; 46% of those earning $100,000 to $200,000; and 23% of those with incomes of $75,000 to $100,000—projects a study by Jerry Tempalski, an economist working at the Treasury Department. A tax on fat cats? Scarcely. Tempalski expects that only 17% of returns with incomes above $1 million will pay AMT in 2005.

The AMT is a tax built on somewhat lower rates than the usual income tax but on a much broader base of income, with many deductions unavailable. You calculate your tax both ways—the AMT way and the regular way—and pay the higher of the two amounts. Some of the differences in the way net income is defined are predictable; the depletion allowance on an oil well can't be used in calculating AMT. Some of them are surprising. Folks who deduct high state and local taxes or claim miscellaneous itemized deductions, including unreimbursed employee business expenses, investment fees and, yes, tax preparation fees, are at risk, since the AMT disallows these, too. Those who take large capital gains, as did Wysocki, are in peril, particularly if they live in a high-tax state like California, as he does. Owners of partnerships, S corporations and limited liability companies can end up in permanent AMT purgatory; these entities pass on to their owners' returns tax breaks such as business credits and depreciation that are either denied or more limited in the AMT. Workers with the kind of stock options handed out to rank-and-file employees can face huge AMT bills and even be bankrupted by those taxes. Americans living abroad are forced to pay AMT on the same income they've already paid stiff foreign taxes on. Some successful tort plaintiffs must pay AMT on money that goes to their lawyers; it is even possible for the tax to be more than the check they get from a successful lawsuit.

In a smaller way the AMT claims many a victim who doesn't even owe it. Anybody who comes close to AMT territory is supposed to calculate taxes both ways. In 1997 seven times as many taxpayers as actually owed AMT had to complete the arduous 54-line "Form 6251, Alternative Minimum Tax." That meant, by the Internal Revenue Service's own figuring, that 63 hours in total taxpayer time was consumed for each tax return showing an AMT liability.

All this torture just to make sure that some rich guys in Texas didn't get off scot-free? Why not just repeal the AMT? No less an institution than the U.S. Treasury proposed just that before the 1986 tax act, but it didn't happen. Repeal is favored now by the IRS' taxpayer advocate, but it won't happen. Congress needs the money brought in by the AMT—an expected $600 billion over the next decade.Sail too close to the AMT and you have a nightmare of tax planning, steering between the Scylla of the regular tax and the Charybdis of the AMT. Suzanne Johnson has been living with this since the mid-1990s, when she started exercising her Intel options and racking up "AMT credits." You get these credits when certain items (some options, for example, but not personal exemptions or state and local taxes) force you to pay AMT. You can use AMT credits to reduce your regular tax liability in any year it exceeds your bill as calculated under the AMT. To claim the credit, you figure your regular tax and AMT each year and then fill out yet another form—the 48-line Form 8801.

Johnson, now 57 and semiretired, meets with Cupertino, Calif. tax adviser Claudia Hill three times a year to plan how to stay out of the AMT and use up her credits. They have whittled more than $140,000 in credits down to $54,813. Every detail counts. When Johnson sells a stock, she quickly moves the proceeds out of the California Municipal Money Fund into which Charles Schwab sweeps the cash. That's because 21% of the fund's 2001 income was taxable for AMT. So much for what used to be called "tax-free bond interest." Despite her efforts, high California taxes and $20,000 in medical and health insurance expenses left Johnson owing $3,000 in AMT for 2001. (Under the regular tax, medical costs exceeding 7.5% of adjusted gross income are deductible; under the AMT, only costs exceeding 10% can be deducted.) Now she's moving from Silicon Valley to state-income-tax-free Nevada. As a scientist, Johnson says, she's frustrated by the AMT's lack of logic and by the failure of the IRS, which issues 340 publications, to offer a pamphlet explaining it. "Taxation without documentation," she grumbles.

How did this obscure tax get to be such a money-raiser? The big tax change in 1986 lowered regular rates and indexed the brackets for inflation. The AMT's exemption, now $49,000 for a couple, is not indexed. (In fact, under current law, it's scheduled to drop to $45,000 for a couple in 2005.)

Thanks to the 1986 act, inflation and income growth alone would be pushing more people into the AMT. But in the last five years, the politicians have made a bad situation worse. They've wooed voters with new tax credits and rate cuts, while cynically relying on the AMT, operating mysteriously and voraciously in the background, to snatch back these breaks and hold down their costs. Last year's tax cut of $1.35 trillion over ten years would have cost $1.7 trillion if it weren't for the AMT.

Taxpayers who use too many deductions, exemptions and credits find that their regular tax drops below the AMT amount. Once they are past that point, any further use of the offending tax advantages does them no good. That's how the nurse from Massachusetts got into the AMT swamp. She had six kids still at home, each supposedly worth one exemption, plus deductions for state and local taxes and nurse's uniforms.

Can you protect yourself? Study these trouble points.

STATE AND LOCAL TAXES

Half the dollar value of tax breaks lost under the AMT in 2000 came from state and local taxes, which aren't deductible in AMT. Some of this pain was avoidable.

Robert Burger retired from a management job at Massachusetts Mutual Life in mid-1999. With payroll withholding stopped, the Hampden, Mass. resident underpaid his 1999 state taxes. He wrote a check for the balance in early 2000 and ended up with a total of $13,400 in state and local taxes to deduct on his 2000 federal return, against a retirement income of just $85,000. The result: $521 in unnecessary AMT. When Burger, who had always done his own taxes, consulted Springfield CPA Richard Moriarty, he found that he could have avoided it by paying all his 1999 state taxes in 1999.

The lesson here is that you usually have a better chance of avoiding or reducing the AMT by matching income and deductions; take large state and local deductions in years when your income is large, too. There are exceptions to this rule, of course. So if you're in AMT territory, or have a sudden change in income, pay an accountant to run the numbers. You might even come out ahead paying your state taxes late—despite a penalty.Sandra Rittenhouse, a Pasadena, Calif. CPA, found herself in an AMT fix last year when, as part of a divorce settlement, she had to pay a big bill for back real estate taxes. Rather than lose the deduction to AMT, she boosted her overall taxable income and reduced her AMT by converting $100,000 from a regular IRA to a Roth IRA. In effect, Rittenhouse reduced the tax rate on the conversion by offsetting the IRA income with a deduction she would otherwise have forfeited. Unhappily, most AMT payers don't have this option; those earning more than $100,000 aren't eligible for Roth conversions.

CAPITAL PAINS

You could be fooled. The special 20% rate for long-term capital gains applies for both regular tax and AMT. So it would seem that adding a capital gain to your income can't change whether you owe AMT or how much.

Paradoxically, capital gains do push people into AMT territory. Case in point: Bill and Hillary Clinton paid $4,943 of AMT in 1999; if their blind trust hadn't taken $122,000 of long-term capital gains, they wouldn't have owed AMT, according to a recalculation of their tax for FORBES by CCH Inc.

What gives? The problem has to do with the fact that a 20% tax rate written into the law turns into something else again on your tax return. Note that, despite their favored tax rate, capital gains count in full in measuring adjusted gross income. AGI, in turn, affects how much of your $49,000 AMT exemption survives a phaseout. The result is that effective rates are often much higher than stated rates. In some parts of the country, an AMT sufferer could pay a combined federal/state tax rate on cap gains of 36%, compared with a 26% combined rate for a taxpayer who isn't in AMT. So calculates Bernard Kent, head of Price-waterhouseCoopers' Midwest financial planning practice.

One defensive tactic used by Kent's clients: They move to Florida, which has no state income tax, before selling their businesses. David Lifson, a partner with Hays & Co. in New York, suggests clients who agree to "installment sales" of their business arrange for payments to be made every other year. Assuming they have other ordinary income, this tactic allows them to stay out of AMT in alternate years. They then crowd their state tax payments into the non-AMT years.

Susan Wheeler, a 49-year-old marketing consultant in St. Paul, had $450,000 in gains in one stock, representing half her portfolio. She turned to Laura Kuntz, a CPA and financial planner with Raymond James, for help diversifying. They devised a three-year strategy. Last year, for example, Wheeler recognized $65,000 in gain, bringing her to the cusp of AMT.

THE EMPLOYEE TRAP

Harold Nicholas was supporting two daughters from his business repairing X-ray machines, netting around $50,000 a year. Then the IRS demanded $7,000 in extra taxes and penalties, plus interest. The problem: The IRS decided that for three years Nicholas had technically been an employee of a partnership he set up with some doctors. Before his deal with the docs, Nicholas deducted expenses for his tools, truck and home-based repair shop on a Schedule C for self-employed taxpayers. But employees get no Schedule C; for them the very same tool costs become a "miscellaneous" deduction. Under the AMT, miscellaneous deductions are for fat cats.

Nicholas shelled out $5,000 for lawyers and accountants to take the case to Tax Court, where he lost. Could he deduct the $5,000? Not in the AMT—legal costs are also "miscellaneous." (Fortunately, he paid the $5,000 in a year he wasn't in the AMT.)Moral: If you pay your own expenses and run your own operation, make sure you take the right steps to qualify as an independent contractor. Anthony D'Acquisto, a Chicago actor who does voiceovers in commercials, paid $18,000 in agent commissions, which helped push him into AMT, and argued in court that he should be able to deduct these expenses on Schedule C. But the court found he was an employee, albeit with many employers, since each individual employer controlled how he did his job.

A solution for D'Acquisto and others in similar situations is to form a personal-service corporation and become its employee. The employers then contract with your corporation. It's a paperwork-intensive solution that can cost from $5,000 to $15,000 a year, Lifson says.

The service corporation won't pass muster with the IRS if you have just one full-time employer. In that case, lobby your boss to pay expenses directly or to reimburse you through an "accountable plan," which requires you to substantiate expenses submitted to your employer. Accountable plan payments don't count as income to employees; flat-rate expense checks do.

THE CREDIT CATCH

Congress has created tax credits for everything from investment in low-income housing to hiring the disadvantaged, (Government By Tax Credit). Yet most such credits can't be claimed against the AMT. Merrick, N.Y. accountant William Stevenson has $18,000 in low-income-housing credits he hasn't been able to use because of the AMT.

"Congress designs this program to get people to invest in housing projects, and then there's this gotcha," he fumes. If you're thinking of investing in one of these deals, think twice. The credits are claimed over ten years and can't be used to reduce your taxes below the AMT level, although they can be carried forward. Can you really be sure you won't be in AMT in the next decade? In some cases you (or a business you control) have a choice between a credit and a seemingly lower-powered deduction. If you are regularly in AMT-land, you'll likely be better off with the deduction.

Not just business and investment credits create trouble. In 2004 and later, people claiming credits for dependent care or college tuition will be at risk of getting a whack from the AMT. To analyze your AMT risk, click here

ICED BY ISOS

"Urgent!! We intend to levy on certain assets. Please respond NOW." Nina Doherty, 39, carries that IRS letter in her purse as a reminder of her $110,000 tax debt. The mother of three stays awake at night wondering what the IRS will take: her Chantilly, Va. house, the $50,000 in her 401(k) or her 1995 Infiniti. While the IRS is making few seizures these days, it is also cutting no special breaks for the thousands of employees like Doherty who were granted "incentive stock options" and through bad advice, bad luck or greed dug themselves into a deep AMT hole.

The key is this: If you exercise an ISO and do not sell the stock before the end of the calendar year, you owe AMT on the difference between what you paid for the stock and what it was worth at the time you exercised. In March 2000 Doherty paid 14 cents a share for 20,000 shares of Net2000 Communications, then valued at $20 a share. By the end of 2000 the stock in the company, which later went into bankruptcy, was trading at $1. Doherty says a broker and co-workers encouraged her to hold on. That made her liable for AMT on $397,200. If she had sold on Dec. 31, she would have owed ordinary income tax instead, but on just $17,200—the spread between the $2,800 she paid for the stock and $20,000.

Moral: If you have a fair amount of ISO stock, don't be led down a garden path by the hope of holding all your stock for a year and converting ordinary income on the position into a favorably taxed capital gain. Even if the stock holds up, you still have the AMT hanging over your head. To play it safe, sell ISO stock soon after exercise.

Or, if you want to play the holding game, exercise the options in January and consult with a tax adviser by December. Chicago tax lawyer Kaye Thomas, author of *Consider Your Options*, suggests this strategy to ISO holders who believe in their companies: Sell enough stock in the year you exercise to cover the ordinary tax on what you've sold, plus the AMT on what you hold. That allows you to profit if the stock climbs, while protecting you from a tax disaster if it tanks.

Doherty notes a cruel irony: Since employers don't report the exercise of ISOs to the IRS, some employees avoided AMT by not reporting their exercise of options to the IRS. "It's the honest people who are getting hurt," she laments.

FAMILY LIFE

The $600 child credit is protected from the AMT, but the $3,000 personal exemption is not. So, if your children are of college age, and you're persistently paying AMT, it may make sense to make them financially "independent" so they can claim personal exemptions and/or college credits on their own returns.

This takes some doing. If you are eligible for an exemption on a child, the child cannot claim an exemption on his own return even if you forgo the exemption or discover that it is worthless to you. So make the children ineligible. You do that by having the youngsters provide more than half their own support. To that end, you give the kids stock before they go off to college. They sell it the next year, at a gains rate as low as 8%, to pay at least half their bills. Note: This maneuver can also work for parents whose exemptions are phased out in the regular tax.

Beware: If your family qualifies for college financial aid, this strategy could backfire. And make sure your "independent" child can still be covered by your health insurance. Exemption planning is also a consideration in divorce. Normally, the custodial parent gets to claim exemptions for the kids, but the IRS allows the exemption to be swapped between parents as part of a divorce deal.

The AMT also sets a trap for newly separated couples. Couples who lived apart for less than six months of the tax year, but weren't yet divorced, are required to file jointly or use the "married filing separately" status. A taxpayer filing this way gets an AMT exemption of only $24,500 for 2002. Last year a recently separated Maryland woman, with five kids and an income of $45,000, found she owed $1,850 in AMT for 2000, says Rockville, Md. CPA Dianne Shangold, who did her returns. So if you're planning on splitting up, do it before July 1.

TREATY? WHAT TREATY?

Thomas Kappus, 54, moved to Toronto in 1972 to expand his family's U.S. restaurant supply business. In 1997 Kappus paid $114,235 (U.S.) of Canadian tax on $244,000 in taxable income, a 47% tax rate. But in February the U.S. Tax Court ruled that despite a U.S.-Canadian tax treaty to prevent double taxation, Kappus still owed $6,152 in U.S. AMT for that year. His bill for subsequent years, Kappus says, will be even bigger. When it toughened the AMT in 1986, Congress decided that the foreign tax credit should eliminate only 90% of AMT. But Revenue Canada holds that this contravenes the treaty and won't give U.S. citizens living in Canada a credit against their Canadian taxes for AMT paid on Canadian income.

"I'd hate to renounce my U.S. citizenship, but this is double taxation defined," says Kappus, who is appealing. "Nobody living in Canada would ever call Canada a tax shelter," he adds.

Our advice: If you are now, or might soon be, exposed to the AMT, get some expert help. You can get a sense of the danger you're in from the free AMT calculator offered by Intuit.

CHAPTER 1

1 Michael Forsythe and Mark Drajem. "A two-century sweet deal may end: The U.S. sugar industry could lose the quotas and supports that keep consumer prices high." *Philadelphia Inquirer*, January 25, 2005, C4.

2 GAO. "Internal Revenue Service: Challenges Remain in Combating Abusive Shelters," Testimony before Senate Finance Committee by Michael Brostek, October 21, 2003.

CHAPTER 2

1 Despite the malodorous history of the Stamp Tax, a variation of it reappeared in the 1930s. As part of his notorious, depression-deepening tax increase of 1932, President Herbert Hoover proposed—and Congress enacted—a Stamp Tax on checks. That's right, you had to pay a 2-cent tax—the equivalent of about 30 cents today—each time you wrote a check. The results were predictably baleful: People pulled money out of already beleaguered banks to conduct their daily transactions, thereby helping to precipitate the near-collapse of the American banking system in 1933. Immediately upon taking office, Franklin Roosevelt had to temporarily shut down all of America's banks. Despite the destructive stupidity of that tax, it remained on the books until the end of 1934.

2 A chapter in *The Way the World Works* by Jude Wanniski, a book first published in 1978, chronicles how the crack-up of the stock market in 1929–30 directly

paralleled the legislative history of the Smoot-Hawley tariff. When prospects for the legislation brightened, stock prices plummeted. During those weeks when it appeared that Smoot-Hawley would not be enacted, equities rallied. Then, as now, the performance of stocks is mightily affected by how the markets anticipate the future.

3   Robert Bartley, *Seven Fat Years* (Detroit: Free Press, 1992).

CHAPTER 3

1   Keating, David. "A Taxing Trend: The Rise in Complexity, Forms and Paperwork Burdens" Policy Paper 113, National Taxpayers Union, April 15, 2004. Online at: http://www.ntu.org/main/press.php?PressID=575.

2   *Newsweek*, September 27, 1997.

3   *New York Times*, September 20, 1997.

4   Varoe, Karen P., Nancy B. Lees and Martha L. López. "Rural Latino Families in California are Missing Earned Income Tax Benefits," *California Agriculture*, Jan-Mar 2004, 24-27.

5   Office of Management and Budget. *Performance and Management Assessments, Budget of the United States Government, Fiscal Year 2004*, page 229.

6   David Cay Johnson. *Perfectly Legal: The Covert Campaign to Rig Our Tax System to Benefit the Super Rich and Cheat Everyone Else.* (Portfolio: New York, 2003), 138-139.

7   Scott Moody. "The Cost of Tax Compliance," Tax Foundation: Washington DC.

8   John Thompson. "Have REITS Helped Tame Texas Real Estate?" *Southwest Economy:* Federal Reserve Bank of Dallas: November/December 2002.

9   Tyson Freeman "Easy Money Fuels a New Building Boom," *National Real Estate Investor,* Sept 30, 1999.

10 "1989, S&L crisis took down PSFS, many others." *Philadelphia Business Journal.* August 2, 2002 (Vol. 21, No. 24).

11 Scott Moody. "The Cost of Tax Compliance," Tax Foundation, February 2002. Online at: http://taxfoundation.org/compliance2002.html

12 Edward C. Prescott. "Why Do Americans Work So Much More Than Europeans?" *Federal Reserve Bank of Minneapolis Quarterly Review:* July 2004, Vol. 28, No.1, pp. 2-13.

13 James R. White and Robert F. Dacey. "Assessment of Fiscal Year 2005 Budget Request and 2004 Filing Season Performance," IRS Testimony before Ways and Means Committee: Washington, DC, March 30, 2004, page 3.

14 Leonard Wiener. "Married Couples Should Find Their Tax Burden Has Been Eased," *The Boston Globe,* June 20, 2004, p. C1.

15 Urban-Brookings Tax Policy Center, "Key Points on the Alternative Minimum Tax," January 21, 2004.

16 Janet Novack. "Alternative Minimum Tax Fix? No Rush," Forbes.com.

17 Ibid.

18 Treasury Department. "Toll-Free Tax Law Assistance to Taxpayers Is Professional and Timely, but Improvement Is Needed in the Information Provided," September 2003, page 9.

19 Kerry Hannon, "Seeking Fast Answers on Taxes," *Wall Street Journal*, April 8, 2003.

20 Michael Barone. "Understanding Harry and Ike; The uneasy friendship of Truman and Eisenhower," *The Weekly Standard:* Vol. 7, No. 28, pg 31, April 1, 2002.

21 GAO. "Internal Revenue Service: Challenges Remain in Combating Abusive Shelters," Testimony before Senate Finance Committee by Michael Brostek, October 21, 2003.

22 "The Problem of Corporate Tax Shelters: Discussion, Analysis and Legislative Proposals." Department of the Treasury. Washington, DC, July 1999.

23 Jay Hancock. "Drilling a hole in IRS' tax shelter offensive," *The Baltimore Sun*, October 31, 2004, p1C.

24 Johnson, 257.

25 Citizens for Tax Justice. "Details on the Bush Tax Cuts So Far," Fall 2003. Online at: http://www.ctj.org/pdf/gwbdata.pdf.

CHAPTER 4

1 Citizens for Tax Justice. "Details on the Bush Tax Cuts So Far," Fall 2003. Online at: http://www.ctj.org/pdf/gwbdata.pdf.

2 Critics should see why payouts from Social Security and Roth IRAs, variable annuities and the like, should be tax-free—the money that went into these vehicles was *after-tax* money.

3 Edmund Andrews, "Republicans Try to Dilute Bill on Taxing Corporations," New York Times, October 5, 2004, C1.

CHAPTER 5

1 In this version, the official rate is 23 percent, but, in reality, it is 30 percent. Here's how designers of this version get that 23 percent: The product you buy is taxed at 30 percent. Say the product costs $100. You would pay a sales tax of $30 (30 percent of $100), along with $100 for the item. You would thus owe $130. What designers of this version do is to take the $30 you paid in sales tax and divide that $30 by $130 ($30 ÷ $130), which comes to 23 percent. For purposes of clarity, we'll use 30 percent for our discussion, not 23 percent.

2 Bartlett, Bruce. 1995. "Replacing Federal Taxes With a Sales Tax." *Tax Notes*, 68:8 (August 21): 997-1003.

3 Robert P. Strauss. Testimony before the Subcommittee on Oversight of the House Ways and Means Committee, May 16, 2000.

4 OECD. 1993. *Taxation in OECD Countries*. Paris: Organization for Economic Cooperation and Development.

5 Mikesell, John L. 1996. "A National Sales Tax? Taxing Consumption the American Way." *Tax Notes*, 72:4 (July 22): 525.

6 William Gale. "A Note on the Required Tax Rate in a National Retail Sales Tax: Preliminary Estimates for 2005-2014," *The Brookings Institution*, August 12, 2004.

CHAPTER 6

1 Alexander Pogerorletskiy and Fritz Sollner. "The Russian Tax Reform," *Intereconomics*. May/June 2002, 156-161.

2 Ibid.

3 Alvin Rabushka. *The Flat Tax at Work in Russia: Year Four, January-June*, January 26, 2005.

4 Rabushka.

5 All three Baltic countries in the 1990s adopted currency boards—their domestic currencies are backed 100 percent by hard currencies—thereby minimizing inflation and avoiding the temptation to print too much money for short-term political gains. Their currencies are, for obviously geographic reasons, fixed to the Euro.

6 Central Statistical Bureau: Latvia, Consumer Price Changes.

7 Doing Business in 2005: Removing Obstacles to Growth. World Bank/International Bank for Reconstruction and Development: Washington, DC, 2005.

8 World Bank. Doing Business in 2005: Removing Obstacles to Growth. World Bank/International Bank for Reconstruction and Development: Washington, DC. 2005.

9 Associated Press. "Romanian Government Says IMF OKs Tax Reform," January 4, 2005.

10 Wetherall, Ben. "Budget 2005: Georgian Government Presents Revised Draft Budget, Ratifies Tax Code," *World Markets Analysis*. December 23, 2004.

11 Alvin Rabushka. "The Flat Tax Spreads to Slovakia," www.russianeconomy.org November 3, 2003.

12 Capital gains, excluding the sale of some owner-occupied housing, is added to regular income and is taxed at 19 percent.

13 Reformers must now tackle Slovakia's onerous payroll taxes, among the highest in the Organisation for Economic Cooperation and Development. High payroll levies in Slovakia and other central and eastern European countries help suppress workers' wages.

14 George Melloan. "In Economic Terms at Least, It's a Good World," *The Wall Street Journal*, October 26, 2004, A25.

15 Katinka Barysch. "One year after enlargement," EurActiv.com April 7, 2005.

16 Andrei Grecu. "Flat Tax—The British Case," Adam Smith Institute: London, 2004, 13.

17 Inland Revenue Department.

18 James Gwartney and Robert Lawson. *Ten Consequences of Economic Freedom.* "Freer Economies Grow Faster," NCPA Study No. 268, July 2004.

19 Daniel Mitchell. "Making American Companies More Competitive," Backgrounder 1691, Heritage Foundation: Washington DC, September 25, 2003.

20 Haig Simonian "Austrian tax cuts worry the Germans as jobs disappear," *Financial Times*. June 24, 2004.

21 Juliet O'Neill. "Celtic Tiger Enjoys Tale of Success," *Vancouver Sun*. June 18, 2003.

22 Patricia Sellers. "eBay's Secret." *Fortune*. October 18, 2004, p160.

23 Glenn Hubbard. *The Impact of U.S. Tax Rules on International Competitiveness.* Testimony before House Committee on Ways and Means: Washington, DC, July 30, 2004.

24 How much money will actually come to the U.S. is questionable: Anti-amnesty Treasury bureaucrats are throwing up regulatory roadblocks.

25 Daniel Mitchell. "Making American Companies More Competitive," Heritage Foundation: Washington, September 25, 2003, 8.

26 Ibid.

27 One example: America's railroad industry employed 1.5 million people after World War II. Today that number has dramatically shrunk to about 200,000. Yet our standard of living is infinitely better today than it was after World War II.

28 Everyone has heard of companies that have "offshore" headquarters in places like Bermuda. These firms operate with little more than a mailing address in Bermuda because of the tax advantages it gives them. In other words, by "moving" the company to another country, many firms lower their tax bills, thereby improving their bottom line and staying competitive. Stanley Works attempted to reincorporate in Bermuda in 2002 to save $30 million in taxes. The resulting outcry forced Stanley to scrap its plans. It eventually laid off 1,000 employees. Despite the outcry, about two dozen American companies have reincorporated overseas in recent years.

CHAPTER 7

1 IRS. Individual Income Tax Returns, IRS SOI Bulletin, 2004.

2 Stuart Butler. "Why the Bush Tax Cuts Are No Threat To Philanthropy," Heritage Foundation. March 8, 2001.

3 Ibid.

4 Stacy A. Teicher. "Donations rise, but not for all," *Christian Science Monitor.* June 21, 2004.

5 Giving USA 2004/AAFRC Trust for Philanthropy.

6 Joe Barnett, ed. *Tax Briefing Book.* National Center for Policy Analysis.

7 Ibid.

8 CBO. Capital Gains Taxes and Federal Revenues. October 9, 2002.

9 Ibid.

10 Arthur Laffer. "The Laffer Curve: Past, Present, and Future." Heritage Foundation: Washington, 2004, 10.

11 IRS. SOI Bulletin.

12 IRS. SOI Bulletin, Historical Table, Summer 2004.

13 Robert Hall and Alvin Rabushka. The Flat Tax. 2nd Ed., Hoover Institution Press: Stanford, 1995.

14 Barry Ritholtz. Understanding Accelerated Depreciation," Maxim Group Special Report, Sept 1, 2004.

ADDITIONAL WRITINGS BY STEVE FORBES:

Fact and Comment (1974), Editor

Some Call It Greed (1977 Filmscript), co-Author

The Moral Basis of a Free Society (1999)

A New Birth of Freedom (1999)